M000290455

FABRICATING ARCHITECTURE

Fabricating
ARCHITECTURE

SELECTED
READINGS
IN
DIGITAL
DESIGN
AND
MANUFACTURING

ROBERT CORSER / editor

Princeton Architectural Press

New York

TABLE OF CONTENTS

FOREWORD / Kimo Griggs

A design process that incorporates the full range of digital technologies is a joy to behold. Designers, technical experts, managers, consultants, vendors, clients, potential users, and those who are financing it all, meet in a place that is still new; at least still new to the architecture world. I am reminded—when things tick along smoothly in my own digital practice and teaching—of an image of an eighteenth- or nineteenth-century mill, with well-oiled machinery in the background producing endless quantities of... stuff, and observers in the foreground wearing top hats and holding parasols touring the plant. In a hand-tipped steel-engraved illustration the scene appears quiet, seamless, almost domestic. I almost want a loom in my living room.

The reality is not depicted: the frequently loud, disorganized, dusty, and dangerous places populated by underpaid labor who spend their days in discomfort. This is not too far from what my own practice and teaching feel like when the digital technologies I have come to rely on suddenly don't work. Surprising amounts of time end up invested in this still-fresh digital realm. Despite our prognostications and declarations regarding the bright promise of a digitally enabled future, it is an often-messy enterprise, requiring an immense amount of machinery, networking, good manners, endless patience, and focused labor to bring about even a modestly successful project; but has it ever been otherwise?

Architects come late to digital technologies, and for good reason. For most of us the necessary equipment was simply too expensive; the military contractors, stone cutters, automotive and product manufacturers, and others who funded the first generations of digital practice predicated their purchases on future efficiencies that we weren't figuring into our practices. Then there was the software: it didn't look good on the screen, and didn't produce the documents that we needed. Finally, there was endless trouble when information needed to be transferred—different "environments" found different ways to define geometries that could not be accurately deciphered in other "environments." During that era I began my own investigations using a large-format computer numerically controlled (CNC) router controlled by disk operating system (DOS) software, with geometries produced in AutoCAD Version 8. I remember it well, and shudder. I had to define ellipses in my manufacturing rather than my drawing software because the geometry wasn't transferable.

Costs came down. Software became friendlier, and file formats were better defined to allow perfect sharing across a variety of platforms. Laser cutters and cost-effective three-dimensional printing in many schools followed almost immediately, fueling students' dreamy expectations without the realities of manufacturing at real scales using real materials. That, too, was soon taken up by those who were engaged in real-life digital practices, and then by students—including the editor during his studies at the Harvard Graduate School of Design (GSD)—through full-scale digital design and fabrication.

At almost the same moment that architects adopted digital fabrication, the image on the screen became precise and colorful. Complex geometries immediately entered our collective consciousness, brought to us by software intended for animation and the design of transportation and infrastructure. Building design and the shape of automotive dashboards and clock radios became practically indistinguishable in some realms. Designing with complex geometries is fun, it is heady, it has led to some remarkable and inspiring work, and as you read between the lines of the following articles, you will note that it can also be deeply problematic.

Fully-integrated digital design–based practice is now perhaps a necessity, and impacts us in many ways; without it architects may soon be dead in the water; with it the way we work is permanently transformed. What changes are taking place, who determines these changes, how these changes will ultimately be made and properly taught to those who will work in the still-being-determined digital environment are consequential questions. It will take time to answer them properly and mistakes are going to be made.

It isn't clear whether we chose this way to practice, whether it chose us, or, honestly, whether we are simply buying into a system that helps others take advantage of our good nature. It is clear, however, that there is power in the new technologies, and that this power must be wielded responsibly.

Kimo Griggs is an architect, fabricator, and educator currently teaching at the University of Washington. He has taught architecture at Yale and Harvard, where he cohosted the first symposiums on CAD/CAM in design and architecture. He coauthored the textbook, *Digital Design and Manufacturing in Architecture and Design*, and contributed the Digital Manufacturing section of *Architectural Graphic Standards*. Along with his architecture practice, he runs a design and fabrication company called Kimo, Inc.

ACKNOWLEDGMENTS

Though this is admittedly a modest project, many groups and individuals contributed immensely to its production. First, I am grateful for the financial and logistical support provided by the University of Washington College of Built Environments and the Department of Architecture. To the authors, editors, and publishers of the essays, I owe a special debt of gratitude for their willingness and assistance in republishing their material. Among these I would especially like to thank the Harvard Graduate School of Design, William Saunders, and Martin Bechthold. Thanks to my colleague Kimo Griggs for his insights and contributions, and to the helpful folks at numerous firms including: Arup, Foster and Partners, Gehry Technologies, KieranTimberlake, Kohn Pedersen Fox Associates, William Massie Architecture, and SHoP Architects. Finally, deepest gratitude is owed to my family, especially Ann Huppert, for support and encouragement.

INTRODUCTION

REREADINGS:
LOOKING BACK AT RECENT DISCOURSE IN EMERGING TECHNOLOGIES

Machines will lead to a new order both of work and of leisure.
—LE CORBUSIER, *Towards a New Architecture*

The digital revolution in architectural design and the adoption of CAD/CAM processes in the building industry can be considered as one of the most radical shifts in architectural history concerning their immense formal and procedural implications.
—TUBA KOCATURK AND MARTIJN VELTKAMP, 2005

Throughout the twentieth century, and into the twenty-first, the expectation of radical changes in the field of architecture as a result of technological innovation and the proliferation of new digital tools and techniques has prevailed. Professionals, academics, and students alike have shared in this general sense of anticipation. Still, there remains a great deal of mystery surrounding precisely how this revolution might reshape architectural practice and significantly impact the built environment.

Outside of highly specialized practices and academic research, the digital revolution has been slow in coming. With the increasing speed and power of personal computers and the decreasing cost of specialized tools like building information and engineering analysis software, laser cutters, and computer numerically controlled (CNC) routers, architects have a growing toolkit of digital design and manufacturing resources at their disposal. But can the availability of new technologies really be expected to bring about a true revolution in the field of architecture?

In the social sciences over the past several decades a distinct field of inquiry has emerged dedicated to evaluating the dynamics of technology's role in social, economic, and cultural change. Scholars typically base their work in opposition to the widely held belief that technological innovations are autonomous drivers of other phenomena—a belief with roots in the Enlightenment that has held sway for most of the twentieth century. In their essay "The Social Shaping of Technology," authors Robin Williams and David Edge observe that many contemporary scholars "are united by an insistence that the 'black-box' of technology must be opened, to allow the socioeconomic patterns embedded in both the content of technologies and the processes of innovation to be exposed and analysed."[1] Rather than being the inevitable result of predictable and immutable forces, the authors describe technological innovation as a "garden of forking paths," with different possible outcomes latent within each new development.[2]

Many noteworthy books document the growing field of digital design and manufacturing in architecture, and all of them seem to underscore the radicalness of these experiments as harbingers of a new paradigm. Yet, few of these books adequately address the truly broad range of issues that underpin, or grow out of, the technological innovations currently at play. In the preface to his important and widely read book *Architecture in the Digital Age*, Branko Kolarevic tells his readers that the projects included "should be seen as bellwethers of the current digital evolution in architecture, and as harbingers of its postdigital future."[3] While his book is born of the implication that there is a digital revolution afoot, and none of the projects or essays included explicitly challenge the idea of a paradigm shift, it is noteworthy that he chose the more nuanced "evolution" rather than revolution, in his introduction. While the preponderance of writing on digital design in architecture over the past decade participates in the rhetoric of revolutionary change, a careful rereading of the body of material at hand reveals a number of more nuanced approaches. This collection of essays is intended to provide an introduction and overview of many of the different manifestations of digital innovation in architecture, but more importantly, it also strives to pose a series of questions regarding the various paths that this digital evolution might take.

Digital Design and Manufacturing in Architecture: An Overview

Beginning in the 1940s the U.S. Air Force developed the earliest numerical control systems for the accurate and repeatable fabrication of aircraft components. Although consisting simply of a series of machine operations encoded on punched paper tape that controlled the functions of industrial machine tools, these techniques represented a revolution in manufacturing and were quickly adopted by other industries. In the 1960s digital computers began finding their way into the design of aircraft and soon thereafter computers began to replace paper tape on the shop floor. In the 1970s and '80s, the linkage of computer-aided design (CAD) and computer-aided manufacturing (CAM) was adopted by other industries for the production of complex products like ships and automobiles. Although initially affordable for only big-ticket or high-volume products, rapid increases in computer power at ever decreasing costs eventually led to the proliferation in CAD/CAM and CNC fabrication in other areas of industrial design and manufacturing.

Notoriously conservative and faced with narrow profit margins on largely one-off projects, the building industry has been slow in adopting these new technologies, except where applicable to produce clear efficiencies in preexisting business processes: the use of CAD in the production of two-dimensional construction documents, for example. Starting in the mid-1990s, however, three powerful forces began to emerge that are starting to transform significant aspects of both design practice and project delivery: intelligent, feature-based parametric modeling; building information modeling (BIM); and mass-customization. Each is based on the primacy of the "master" building model as the repository of both design intent and highly specific product information. Combined with the ability to use numerically controlled processes to directly implement this digital data for the actual construction of buildings, information technologies are undeniably of growing importance. As these technologies become more widespread and affordable, their promise of faster, more flexible, and more cost-effective building processes is beginning to be realized in the architectural, engineering, and construction industries. Although the long-term implications for this kind of technological shift remains subject to debate, their outlines are certainly visible in the essays chosen for inclusion in this volume.

The "Processes" section of this book starts with an overview of different approaches to digital design and fabrication in architecture. The first essay, by Achim Menges entitled "Instrumental Geometry," is based on discussions with the founding members of the SmartGeometry Group, a London-based consortium of groundbreaking pioneers of digital design in architecture whose stated goal is to "create the intellectual foundations for a more profound way of designing." In his "Using Building Information Modeling for Performance-based Design," architect Eddy Krygiel outlines the well-known advantages of BIM in creating project efficiencies and provides case studies of how this new technology can to be integrated with performance analysis tools to aid designers in creating more sustainable buildings. From this focus on digital modeling's potential to control geometry and integrate with performance analysis, the topic shifts to issues surrounding the manufacture and construction of digitally generated designs. "Innovate or Perish," written by David Celento, provides an economic and cultural critique of "business as usual" in architecture and argues for the adoption of new tools and new building methods. This essay serves as both a broad overview of technologies and tools that are becoming available and a compelling call for a revolutionary, rather than evolutionary, digital transformation of architectural practice.

"Practices," the second section of this book, presents essays describing noteworthy design practices that test and deploy new digital technologies in a broad spectrum of applications. The first essay, "CAD/CAM in the Business of Architecture, Engineering, and Construction," features an interview with James Glymph, a partner at Gehry Partners and chief executive officer of Gehry Technologies. It focuses on the ramifications of digital design and fabrication for professional practice. Among the important questions Glymph addresses are the increasingly blurred lines of ownership and responsibility for digital information during the design and construction processes and the challenges of "rethinking the procurement process" required to fully exploit CAD/CAM's advantages. The second essay focuses on the work of the New York–based firm SHoP Architects, leading innovators in the use of digital technologies, whose unique digital design-build process has transformed the shape of architectural practice today. "Remaking in a Postprocessed Culture" presents the work and philosophy of William Massie, an important educator and practitioner of digital design and fabrication. According to Massie, "When an author produces a drawing which becomes the information that drives the machine, it compresses the world of design and fabrication into a single process," resulting in what he claims—and his work shows to be—a "substantial increase in artistic autonomy."

The challenges faced by engineers who collaborate with innovative architects such as Massie in the production of digitally based designs are addressed in the essay "Engineering of Freeform Architecture," by Harald Kloft, principal of o-s-d, the office for structural design in Frankfurt, Germany. Based on his particular experience working with architects Bernhard Franken, Frank Gehry, Peter Cook, and others, Kloft identifies the challenges of geometry creation and resolution, data transfer, and structural analysis. Of particular interest is the topic of structural optimization and each architect's relative degree of willingness to alter his formal proposals to address performance and construction issues. And finally, no overview of the impact of new technologies on the building industry would be complete without a discussion of Stephen Kieran and James Timberlake's influential book *Refabricating Architecture*.[4] The last essay in this section on digitally based practices explores this, the first true manifesto for digital design and manufacturing in architecture. According to Kieran and Timberlake, "Today, through the agency of information management tools, the architect can once again become the master builder by integrating the skills and intelligences at the core of architecture (in order to) uphold a true return to craft." It seems clear from these examples of CAD/CAM's early adoption at all levels of design practice that digital technologies are poised to exert a major influence on architecture. But how will the design and construction industries respond? And what are the implications for a digitally based design culture? As authors Willis and Woodward point out in their essay at the end of this collection, "Revolutions…are notoriously difficult to predict."

The last part of this collection, "Reactions and Projections," seeks to widen the discussion of emerging technologies and to document some important questions that are being asked from a number of different points of view. Since discussions of CAD/CAM typically bias form generation and data management, it seems fruitful to ask about the other side of the fabrication equation and delve into issues of materiality. In "Self-organisation and Material Constructions," Michael Weinstock, academic head of the Architectural Association School of Architecture in London, discusses the role of new materials and materials science in the digital revolution through the development of foamed polymers, metals, and ceramics. After analyzing the self-organizing characteristics of natural systems such as space-filling polyhedra and foam geometries, he concludes by identifying an ongoing "systematic change" in design whereby eventually, "the boundary between the 'natural' and the 'manufactured' will no longer exist."

The final three essays in this collection call for further critiques of digital technologies' potential. In his "Automation Takes Command," architect, author, and educator Kiel Moe provides a cogent summary of the socio-cultural factors underpinning the development of numerically controlled manufacturing processes as a basis for challenging readers to consider whether new developments in this area truly represent the kind of revolution that many proponents claim. In "On Shells and Blobs," Martin Bechthold, professor of architectural technology at Harvard's Graduate School of Design, addresses the lack of structural sophistication in much contemporary "blob" architecture and argues for the investigation of structurally efficient predigital systems like thin-shell concrete.

In their essay "Diminishing Difficulty," architect Todd Willis and Pennsylvania State University architecture professor Daniel

Woodhouse critically address widespread claims about the industry-changing potential of CAD/CAM and mass-customization, taking particular aim at Kieran and Timberlake's book *Refabricating Architecture*. Their central concern is the "gap" between the digital model and the real building that it anticipates. Some suggest that with ever more precise digital modeling this gap will cease to exist. Yet others maintain that the complexities of material reality like thermal expansion, for example, or material grain, will forever require the kind of accommodation (and opportunity) discussed by Robin Evans in his important 1997 essay "Translations from Drawing to Building."[5] Woodhouse and Willis question Kieran and Timberlake's assertion that "the difficulty of producing architecture will be diminished by reordering practice around 'information.'" Instead, they posit "difficulty as a source of architectural value" by virtue of the importance of architecture's productive "resistance" to "material, climatic, economic (and) social" forces. Without dismissing the importance—or even the inevitable impact—of new digital technologies on architecture, the authors ask provocative questions about how architects might integrate new digital technologies with practices that acknowledge and maintain all the crucial but messy aspects of architecture—aspects that *resist* digital quantification and optimization.

The majority of essays presented in this collection appeared in print, in English, between 2001 and 2008. A small number of previously unpublished essays have also been included to broaden the critical debate or to fill gaps in the literature. Digital design and digital manufacturing are equal players in the productive confluence of information technology and craft, and a preference for approaches that address both digital and material aspects of architecture guided the selection of essays for inclusion.

The resulting collection provides an overview of the numerous manifestations of digital innovation in architecture. It would surely be possible to devote a similar number of pages to any one of the individual approaches to digital design treated herein. Building information modeling, for example, has received a great deal of attention lately in the architectural press, and the application of parametric, geometric, and algorithmic computation to form generation could similarly be the subject of several volumes of collected essays. What this particular volume aims for is not comprehensive coverage but rather, an incisive cross-sectioning of the body of recent literature that documents the convergence of digital design and digitally controlled manufacturing in the architecture, engineering, and construction industries. Due to the speed of developments in both technology and practice, it is likely that an updated edition will be needed before long. What is hoped, however, is that this collection will provide an informative and pro-vocative sampling of the rich discourse that is taking place today, dur-ing an important moment of evolutionary transformation in the field of architecture.

Notes

Epigraph 1 Le Corbusier, *Towards a New Architecture* (London: John Rodker, 1927; New York: Dover Publications, 1986), 101. Citation is to the Dover edition.

Epigraph 2 Tuba Kocaturk and Martijn Veltkamp, "Interdisciplinary Knowledge Modelling for Free-Form Design—An Educational Experiment," *Computer Aided Architectural Design Futures 2005*, Proceedings of the 11th International CAAD Futures Conference held at the Vienna University of Technology, Vienna, (2005): 465.

1 Robin Williams and David Edge, "The Social Shaping of Technology," *Research Policy* 25, no. 6 (1996): 865.

2 Ibid., 866.

3 Branko Kolarevic, *Architecture in the Digital Age: Design and Manufacturing* (New York: Taylor & Francis, 2005), v.

4 Stephen Kieran and James Timberlake, *Refabricating Architecture: How Manufacturing Methodologies Are Poised to Transform Building Construction* (New York: McGraw-Hill, 2004).

5 Robin Evans, *Translations from Drawing to Building and Other Essays* (London: Architectural Association, 1997).

PART ONE

PROCESSES:
NEW AGENDAS
FOR DIGITAL
TOOLS IN
ARCHITECTURAL
PRACTICE

INSTRUMENTAL GEOMETRY

Achim Menges

This essay is structured around conversations with the founding members of the SmartGeometry Group, a London-based collaboration between groundbreaking pioneers of digital design in architecture whose stated goal is to "create the intellectual foundations for a more profound way of designing." Menges establishes the background of technology transfer from other industries, and defines key terms such as parametric design, mass-customization, *and* object-oriented, feature-based modeling. *The SmartGeometry Group members are leaders in software development, research, and design. They discuss new developments in digital design environments, collaboration between different design disciplines, and emerging trends in digitally manufactured building systems as illustrated in case studies, which include Foster and Partners' designs for the Smithsonian Institution Courtyard roof (2004–2007) and the Kohn Pedersen Fox Associates' (KPF) Bishopsgate Tower project (2005, unbuilt) in London. These projects demonstrate the use of parametric design and rigorous geometry in the development and construction of complex building forms and systems.*

Geometry has always played a central role in architectural discourse. In recent years, the importance of geometry has been reemphasized by significant advances in computer-aided design (CAD) and the advent of digital fabrication and performance analysis methods. New design approaches are being developed that will profoundly change the current nature and established hierarchies of architectural practice. The arrival of parametric digital modeling changes digital representations of architectural design from explicit geometric notation to instrumental geometric relationships. Architects are beginning to shift away from primarily designing the specific shape of a building to setting up geometric relationships and principles described through parametric equations that can derive particular design instances as a response to specific variables, expressions, conditional statements, and scripts.

Robert Aish, Lars Hesselgren, J. Parrish, and Hugh Whitehead have been at the forefront of these developments for many years. The formative period for their collaboration, when the intent and methodology of parametric design applied to architecture was established, was the time when all of them were working for, or in collaboration with, Yorke Rosenberg Mardall (YRM) in the mid-1980s. There they took Intergraph's Vehicle Design System and applied it to pioneering buildings such as the Waterloo International Rail Terminal (1994) by Nicholas Grimshaw and Partners and the "Stadium for the Nineties," a project that featured a retractable roof defined through fully associative geometry. Since then, Robert Aish has moved on to become director of research at Bentley Systems, where he is responsible for the development of new parametric design software. Lars Hesselgren is director of research and development at KPF London, where he has been involved with many major building projects, most recently the Bishopsgate Tower. Hugh Whitehead leads the Specialist Modeling Group at Foster and Partners that has provided consultancy on such prominent buildings as the Swiss Re Tower (2003), Greater London Authority City Hall (2002), the Sage Gateshead (2004), and Beijing Airport (2003–2008). J. Parrish, director of ArupSport, has contributed to the development of outstanding sports stadiums such as the Sydney Olympic Stadium (1999) and the Allianz Arena (2005) in Munich. Together they formed the SmartGeometry Group, and here they outline their common views on the aim of the group.

"The objective of the SmartGeometry Group," says Lars Hesselgren, is to create the intellectual foundations for a more profound way of designing. Change can only be additive, not subtractive, so SmartGeometry does not reject or deny existing, more informal, or intuitive approaches to design. What SmartGeometry initially set out to achieve was to add to the established skills other complementary formal systems of notation that would allow for the creation and control of more complex geometry. We recognized that architecture, and design in the broadest sense, was critically dependent on geometry, but that a complete geometric tradition of the understanding of descriptive and construct geometry was being lost through lack of use in a bland planar and orthogonal minimalism or, indeed, through misuse by being excessively indulged at the "hyper" fringes of design. Against this background, the objective of the SmartGeometry Group was to reassert an understanding of geometry in design as more than an "experiential commodity." Rather than being willful and arbitrary, even the most complex geometry could provide a formal resolution of competing forces and requirements. It could suggest and resolve both structural efficiency and environmental sensitivity.

He summarizes the group's active engagement in building up new skills and techniques for current and future generations of architects: "The group aims to help create the intellectual environment for further developments in this field that stretch beyond relatively simple geometric mechanisms into more complex approaches to the generation and evaluation of built forms."

In pursuing an instrumental understanding of geometry, the group identified very early on the limits of "conventional" CAD concepts that mimic pen and paper with mouse and screen, and constrain the architectural language through libraries of predetermined architectural elements. Robert Aish explains,

There was a direct mapping between what was thought to be an architectural vocabulary of: "walls, windows, and doors" and a simplified computational equivalent. Maybe this was all that could be implemented at the time. But the net result, and disastrous at that, was to entrench this highly limited form of architecture by making it "more efficient" and excluding to architecture based on more general geometry or less conventional components and configurations. What is different with recent parametric design tools is that the set of constructs is far more abstract, but at the same time the system is "extensible," so that it is the designer who can make his own vocabulary of components. We have broken the "hard-coded" naive architectural semantics. We are no longer interested in "local efficiency" within a restrictive CAD system, but rather the designer has the opportunity to define his own vocabulary from first principles, by first understanding the underlying geometric and algebraic abstractions.

A parametric approach to design has already been in use in the aero, automotive, naval, and product design industries. In fact, most related software applications are spin-offs from these industries. All of the SmartGeometry members were users or developers of some of the early parametric software for mechanical engineering and naval architecture. Hugh Whitehead and Robert Aish explain their views on concepts of parametric applications in those fields, comparing them to architecture and outlining the group's strategies for developing a new parametric design application as follows:

> Production industries for the engineering of cars, ships, and aircraft are geared to minimize tooling costs by creating a range of standard models from mass-produced custom components. On the other hand, construction industries for the architecture of buildings aim to create one-off custom designs, but with an economy based on the use of standardized components. Of course, this is a simplistic historical view. However, it aims to highlight the different approaches of the two industry sectors. Both achieve a variety of products while exploiting standardization in different ways to achieve efficiency. The advent of digital fabrication techniques has made possible the concept of "mass customization," which is blurring this distinction and thereby allowing industries to learn from each other and also to borrow technologies. But the core technology for the shift resides in software engineering.

The success of a piece of software is about the match or mismatch of assumptions between the software designer and the users. We can say that we all learnt from the assumptions made by the software developers of these other parametric systems for other industries. We learnt about what was transferable to architecture and we learnt what additional functionality would be required if the transition of parametric design to architecture was to be successful. There are two important characteristics of parametric design applied to aircraft or ship design that are not present in terrestrial architecture. The first is that concepts and configurations change relatively slowly. Secondly, a single design, with some minor variations, will be used for a production run of ten, hundreds, or possibly thousands of instances. Therefore, there is the time and resources to invest in the proper "genotype" and ensure that this can support the anticipated variations in the phenotypes. Contrast this with buildings where, in the main, each one is unique. There is no time or need to develop a highly adaptive genotype. There is only one instance so there is no need for a genotype that can support variations in the phenotype.

There are three exceptions to this statement. First, with a building such as a sports stadium, which is distinctly "rule-based," it may be advantageous to develop a strong genotype the characteristics of which can be refined and shared with successive variants. Second, a building such as the Grimshaw Waterloo International Railway Terminal contains "variation" within a single configuration. In this case, establishing a viable genotype for the characteristic "banana" truss was an essential prerequisite for the design. Third, all design can benefit from refinement. We don't just build the first idea. The intellectual processes of externalization, generalization, and abstraction that are essential in aircraft or ship design to define the genotype can also benefit a one-off building design. However, the important difference with terrestrial architecture is the rapid exploration of alternative configurations. This requirement for the convenient exploration of alternative configurations adds an important requirement to the functionality of parametric design tools. Thus it seemed to be of prime importance to create a system with great flexibility, particularly in the form and content of "collections."

Buildings are collections of objects. If the design changes, as it will or should do, then these collections of objects have to respond. The content of the collections will change, and the individual members of the collection also have to respond uniquely to changes in their specific context. If we wish to support a flexible approach to design, then this requires that the concept of flexibility and responsiveness is programmed in from the very initial thoughts about the application, and then this concept has to be consistently implemented. But what this also means is that designers who use this software must understand how to control this type of flexibility, how to think abstractly about design with an "algebra of collections." The question is whether the need to understand and be completely conversant with a formal notation is acceptable to architects and designers. Is it either an essential way to add precision to the expression of design intent or an imposition that distracts from an intuitive sense of design? Historically architecture successfully combined different ways of thinking that spanned both the intuitive and the formal. So there is a strong precedence established. Of late, the formal component has been somewhat lacking, again with notable exceptions. Certainly the emerging architectural practices being started by the new generation of graduates emerging from architectural schools have no inhibitions in moving effortlessly between these two approaches and producing impressive results.

One of the focal points of the group's work in synergizing their individual expertise in a unique collaboration spanning the worlds of practice, research, and education is the development of the GenerativeComponents software. All of the group's members contribute in different ways to the evolution of the software, and they are in agreement that "the specification of GenerativeComponents is intentionally open-ended and generic in order to provide an integrated environment for design and development that is not tied to any specific industry or workflow conventions. It aims to support the evolution of ideas by exposing the language and making this accessible to both designer and developer in a consistent manner at all levels of interaction."

Robert Aish, who is leading the development of Generative-Components as Bentley's director of research, more specifically explains the key concepts of this next generation of CAD software:

We can describe GenerativeComponents as an "object-oriented, feature-based" modeling system and development environment that represents the convergence of design theory with computational theory. The GenerativeComponents technology is based on the following eight key concepts:

1. Implication: the ability to define "long-chain" associativity of geometric constructs, allowing the implications of change to be explored via automatic change propagation

2. Conditional modeling: the ability to encode and exercise alternative implications allowing changes in behavior or configuration of the geometric construct

3. Extensibility: the ability to turn parametric models into new reusable components, where behavior of the component is defined by the original model

4. Components: the transition from digital components representing discrete physical entities to devices for cognitive structuring

5. Replication: the ability to operate on sets of digital components, potentially where each set member can uniquely respond to variations in its context

6. Programmatic design: the ability to combine declarative representations in the form of an implication structure and procedural representations

7. Multiple representations: the ability for the user to simultaneously create and operate on different complementary, linked representations

8. Transactional model of design: representations are an editable, reexecutable design history.

All software is based on the concept of representation, so what is being represented with GenerativeComponents? Superficially, what the user sees on the screen is geometry that might represent some building or other more general design, but this is not the primary representation. At the next level of depth, GenerativeComponents is explicitly modeling the dependency or other more general relationships between geometry and other nongraphic elements such as variables, expressions, conditional statement, and scripts. Again, this is not the primary representation. What is effectively being represented are design decisions or, more correctly, a "transactional" model that allows a sequence of alternative decisions to be constructed, exercised, and evaluated. This corresponds to the process of design at its most fundamental.

Nonetheless, parametric design systems are introducing a whole new set of concepts, based on design theory, computational theory, and object-oriented software engineering that may be quite unfamiliar to practicing designers. Yet the intention of GenerativeComponents is to apply these concepts in a way that is directly related and beneficial to the process of design.

Some of these concepts have already been implemented in practice by members of the group in close collaboration with project-specific design teams. With the aim of exploiting advantages of parametric design processes, new ways of enabling and structuring the development of geometrically complex buildings have been established. Hugh Whitehead explains how such a parametric approach to design has become instrumental for the work of Foster and Partners:

At Foster and Partners the Specialist Modeling Group provides in-house consultancy to project teams at all stages from concept design to detailed fabrication. Although we provide tools, techniques, and workflow, these are developed in the reverse order. Starting with the formulation of the problem, the first step is to propose an appropriate workflow. Within this frame of reference, suitable techniques are tried and tested in different combinations. The results then form the brief for the development of custom tools that are tested by the design team in a continuing dialogue. Custom tool-building ensures that a rationale becomes an integral part of the design concept. This then allows for the generation and control of more complex building geometries.

In addition to the Smithsonian Institute project, another interesting example is the Swiss Re building that forced us to address the problem of how to design and produce details that are programmed rather than drawn. At each floor, the rules are always the same, but the results are always different. At the same time, even if every plan, section, and elevation could have been drawn, this still would not adequately describe the design intent, even for tender purposes let alone construction. The building stands as a classic example of an associative framework providing a context for adaptive parametric components, so that fabrication follows a consistent dialogue between structural and cladding node geometry. The designer is in charge of the rehearsal, but the contractor is responsible for the performance. We are limited in what we can build by what we are able to communicate. Many of the problems we now face are problems of language rather than technology. The experience of Swiss Re established successful procedures for communicating design through a geometry method statement.

Complex geometries involve very large parameter sets that are impossible to control by direct manipulation. With buildings like the Beijing Airport, which has a double-curved roof that is three kilometers long, the approach was to develop control mechanisms that can be driven by law curves. Law curves control "rate of change" and can be geometric as graphs or algebraic as functions. By representing higher derivatives as curves, or even surfaces, complex behavior can be achieved with simple manipulation.

Such a parametric and editable approach to design offers a high degree of geometric control combined with the ability to rapidly generate variations. All of the group's members agree that parametric models therefore seem to be particularly versatile in providing the relevant information for digital performance tests. However, the requirements for different analysis methods need to be considered. Whitehead continues:

Digital performance tests are carried out in collaboration with external consultants. This involves many different software applications and operating systems, but more importantly each requires a different simplified representation of the model as the input to their analysis routines. Structural analysis requires center lines, thermal analysis requires volumes, acoustic analysis requires simple planes, and daylight analysis requires meshes. The more complex and detailed the model, the more difficult it is to decompose to an appropriate level of simplification. Because of the cost of simplifying or rebuilding models, consultants prefer to engineer a design only when the configuration has become stable. However, when the model is generative, it becomes easier to produce multiple representations, which remain associative to the conceptual framework. This ability allows one to track comparative options and to perform more iterations of the analysis cycles. Consequently, the main impact of such an approach on the practice of architecture is on the decision-making process. Previously the designer had to freeze the early strategic decisions in order to progress to increasing levels of detail. This involved cyclic explorations, but the early decisions can only be challenged if there are both time and resources to rework the downstream details. In a parametric approach, the ability to populate an associative framework with adaptive components allows us to defer the decision-making process until we are ready to evaluate the results.

Parametric modeling has been understood as instrumental for its ability in improving workflow, its rapid adaptability to changing input and its delivery of precise geometric data for digital fabrication and performance analysis. But while accelerating and extending established design processes, the skills and techniques developed by the SmartGeometry Group do also inherently challenge the way we think about the design of buildings. One may argue that novel aspects in architecture emerge when deeply entrenched typologies, conventions, and preconceptions of the organization and materialization of the built environment are challenged and rethought by the design team. The SmartGeometry Group envisions their approach to design to become instrumental for such processes of rethinking architecture. Hugh Whitehead explains:

> As of yet, designers use sketches and models to externalize a thought process, in order to provide both focus and stimulus for the development of shared ideas. The use of generative techniques that are

editable promotes a higher level of awareness. It encourages all pre-conceptions to be challenged because they must first be formulated in language.

Robert Aish concludes by highlighting the group's awareness of the importance of developing a culture of use of generative techniques in parallel to the digital tools themselves:

> In general, there is a shift in many human activities from "doing" to "controlling," involving the development of tools and a "culture of use" of these tools. Design as a discipline emerges from the craft process as a way of abstracting and evaluating alternative possible configurations, usage scenarios, and materializations without actually physically making and testing each possible alternative. Design involves many analogues of the finished artifact that, with varying fidelity, simulate or indicate the anticipated behavior of the yet-to-be-built result. These analogues, the design medium, introduce representational and manipulation techniques that may be interesting or attractive in their own right, and these may start to influence the resulting physical outcomes. Seen from this perspective, the development of computational design tools, including parametric tools, may not be too different to development of preceding design tools or to the development of tools in general.
>
> What we need to focus on is the relationship between the development of these tools and the corresponding development of the skills and the culture of use.

Robert Aish, Bentley Systems, GenerativeComponents
Parametric Design Software Development

Design involves both exploration and the resolution of ambiguity. Therefore, it is not sufficient that computational design tools can model a static representation of a design. What is important is that the design tools are able to capture both the underlying design rules from which a range of potential solutions can be explored, and facilitate how this "solution space" can be refined into a suitable candidate for construction. The question is, how can these design rules be represented and how can this exploration and refinement process be supported?

By way of illustration, let us consider the issues involved when a roof, initially based on a doubly curved freeform surface, is required to be constructed from planar components. Here, the designer might want to explore simultaneously two interrelated aspects of the design: alternative surface configurations and alternative penalization strategies.

To model not just one solution to this problem, but the design rules that can be used to explore alternative solutions, requires a complex "graph" of "associative geometry." The system of geometric relationships developed here is quite complex to understand, even when presented with the finished model. It is necessary to imagine how much more complex it was to originate the model. Our contention as software developers is that a 3-D geometric representation, while essential, would be insufficient to describe the complex geometric associativities required to present the underlying design rules. So in addition to the standard geometry model we include a symbolic model that externalizes and presents these relationships in an explicit graphical form. Also represented is a law curve "controller" that provides a geometric input at one stage removed from the geometric models and the flat pattern layout of the panels ready for laser cutting. In this context, the law curve is controlling the elevation profile of the roof surface, independently of the plan "S" configuration of the "spine" curve.

What variations does this model allow us to explore? a) the poles of the spine curve can be moved in Cartesian space; b) the position of the planes on the spine curve can be moved in 1-D parametric space (along the spine curve); c) the poles of the cross-sectional curves can be moved in the 2-D planar space; d) the number and spacing of the points on the surface can be defined within the surface's 2-D parameter space; e) various alternative "lacing" options are available to use the points on the surface to populate either planar or nonplanar quadrilateral or triangular panels; and f) the order of the spine curves and cross-sectional curves can be varied. Having defined this process, the designer can then explore variations within the solution space, not in some rigid parametric way, but by using an intuitive process of "direct manipulation" and "hand-eye coordination."

Here, the designer can graphically select and manipulate one of the control points of the law curve model and observe: a) the law curve update; b) the cross-section curves update; c) the surface update; d) the points on the surface update; e) the quadrilateral panels on the surface update; and f) the planar unfolded fabrication model update. The whole process is being intuitively controlled in dynamics with the designer completely in control of the "form making" process and its material-ization. While these variations are reasonably complex, it should be stressed that they are only the variations that can be explored within this particular logical and geometric configuration. The designer can also change the configuration (by editing the relationships in the sym-bolic model), which then opens up alternative ranges of variations to be explored.

To arrive at this level of expression and control required that the designer had to be skilled in the logic of design, in order to define and refine the complex system of geometric, algebraic, and logical rela-tionships that is the essential foundation of this process. Ultimately, it is this combination of intuition and logic, of ideas and skills, that is of interest.

Hugh Whitehead, Brady Peters, and Francis Aish, Foster and Partners, Specialist Modeling Group, Smithsonian Institution Courtyard Enclosure, Washington DC, 2004

In 2004, Foster and Partners won an invited international architecture competition to design a new courtyard enclosure for the Smithsonian Institution's Patent Office Building in Washington DC. [Fig. 1] Early in the project, the Specialist Modeling Group was brought in to advise the project team on modeling techniques, to develop new digital tools, and help solve the complex geometric issues involved. Norman Foster's early sketch shows a diagonal grid of structural elements gen-tly flowing over the central courtyard. The undulating roof structure is supported by eight columns arranged in three domes, the central peak being the highest and having the greatest span.

Instead of simply translating a sketch, capturing design intent involves the development of a digital schematic that can be easily used by the designers to control and manipulate the complex geom-etry. Design constraints are encoded within a system of associated geometries. Three surfaces, column markers, and a computer script control the entire roof geometry. Constraints such as edge beam loca-tion, dome heights, and drainage locations are informed by the design

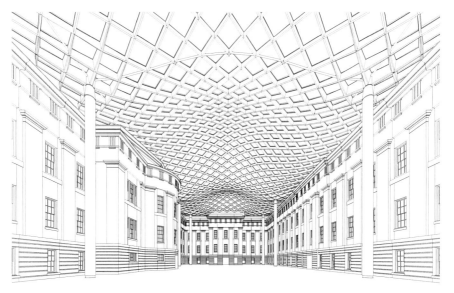

Fig. 1 / Interior study, Smithsonian Institution Courtyard, Foster and Partners, 2004

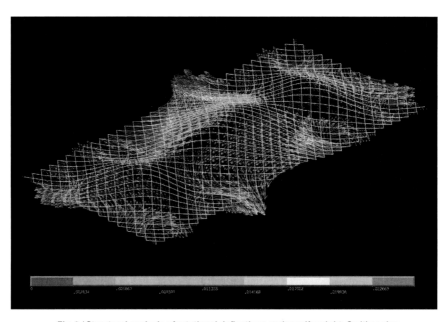

Fig. 2 / Structural analysis of rotational deflections under self-weight, Smithsonian Institution Courtyard, Foster and Partners, 2004

surface, which is created from a series of simple control lines. The parameterization of the grid surface sets out the plan locations of the design nodes, while the height location is given by the design surface. The relationship between these surfaces and a third surface controls the beam twist. The set-out geometry performs as a mechanism to control the parameters of a generative script.

Using the set-out geometry and a set of parameter values, a computer script creates a variety of detailed roof components. The script adapts each component to its local condition and, through a performance evaluation, the components respond to their environment. The use of scripting as a design approach provided many benefits:

1. The simultaneous generation of multiple representations within a single model; a center-line model for structural analysis [Fig. 2]; a triangulated flat-panel model for acoustic analysis; a simplified model for hidden line visualizations; lighting node position models; node and beam set-out drawings and spreadsheets; unfolded beams for the digital fabrication of scale models; and a complete model of all roof elements for the creation of drawings by the project team.

2. The independent development of roof configuration and individual component strategies. The roof geometry was free to change without affecting the logic of the beam section or panelization system. Within the script, different modules of code could be inserted, removed, or edited to create new roof options. Using this approach, the long-chain dependencies of a fully associative system did not exist, and modification was simpler and regeneration much faster. When changes were made to the script or to the set-out geometry, a new digital model could be generated rapidly. A dynamically parametric model was not necessary.

3. A computer-generated model gave very precise control over the values and relationships within the roof system. It produced consistent and repeatable results where the design history was saved as a copy of the generating script and the set-out geometry used.

The design evolution involved the use of many different media and techniques and an intense dialogue between a large team and many consultants. The script became a synthesis of all the design ideas and was constantly modified and adapted during the design process. Scripting was used as a sketching tool to test new ideas. This

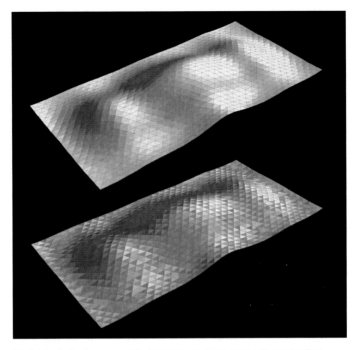

Fig. 3 / Analysis of average daily insolation on roof panels without shading
device (top) and with shading device (bottom), Smithsonian Institute Courtyard,
Foster and Partners, 2004

explorative approach required knowledge of both programming and
architectural design combined with interpretative skills on many levels. It proved a fast and flexible approach. The final version of this
generating code was 5,000 lines in length and had 57 parameters—
some numeric values and others switch—controlling options. Using
only the set-out geometry as input, the script generated approximately
120,000 elements in about fifteen seconds; 415 models were generated over six months.

It is possible to generate thousands of different options by using
scripting. It therefore becomes increasingly important to not only
understand the system constraints, but to have a clear strategy for
evaluating the generated options. The design was evaluated by many
methods: structural, environmental, acoustic, and aesthetic. [Fig. 3]
While there was no attempt to automate the feedback process, it did
prove beneficial to work closely with consultants to better understand

their data-input needs for their analyses. By building the production of this information into the script, the generation/analysis cycle could be shortened. Working closely with the structural engineers, Buro Happold, reduced the time taken for the generation/analysis loop. As well as creating traditional visualizations and animations, a new technique was employed in which an image set was automatically generated and reviewed for a matrix of options. In parallel, the physical production of digitally fabricated scale models and the production of 1:1 mock-ups was critical to the decision-making process.

Lars Hesselgren and Stylianos Dritsas, KPF London, Bishopsgate Tower, City of London, 2005

The Bishopsgate Tower project utilizes only simple geometry—lines and tangent arcs—in order to facilitate manufacture. The footprint polygon is carefully calibrated to fit the site. [Fig.4] The setting out progresses from the root point of the building, and the primary geometry is a set of tapered planes chamfered with sheared cones. The taper on each plane provides the only control mechanism within the geometric system to control the taper of the sheared cones. The helical crown is a solution to the visual problem posed by the viewing of the building from multiple points.

The parametric modeling allowed easy tuning of the exact height of the crown. To achieve natural control of the helical curve in space, a "normalized graph" was built. The visual verification of the crown results in the curve having a slight "S" shape. The essential rule for the structural system is that it is offset from the design skin. Each column has its center-line on a vector that is parallel to the setting-out geometry, with the result that all columns are straight and no column is vertical. The mullions are on a simple module set out linearly from the point of origin and, since the building tapers, the modules are offset, introducing shear in the facade.

To achieve natural ventilation there is an outer glass skin made of flat, planar glass panels of identical size. The panels are tipped in space to create overlaps both in plan and in section, which act as ventilation spaces. The system for establishing correct overlap involved the development of a programmed extension to the parametric system. The selected methodology respects the attitude of a particular panel

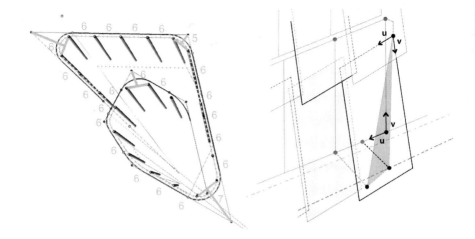

Fig. 4 / **Parametric setup of main columns, Bishopsgate Tower London, Kohn Pedersen Fox London, 2005 (left)**

Fig. 5 / **Planar glass panels of outer skin, Bishopsgate Tower London, Kohn Pedersen Fox London, 2005 (right)**

with respect to its neighbors. [Fig. 5] The canopy is tangential to the main design surface for aesthetic and aerodynamic reasons. The differing requirements along the canopy length, ranging from near-vertical sections to "peaked hat" lift-up sections for protecting and signaling entrances, is solved by an edge curve driven by two law curves. The springing height is horizontal and supports the unique arc, which is tangential at the plane of every planning module vector. Each arc is divided into a harmonic series based on the length of the arc. Each set of points is connected longitudinally forming the center-lines of the canopy "hoops," which are doubly curved in space.

Lars Hesselgren and Neri Oxman, KPF London, Folded-Plate Roof Research Project, 2005

This project is a research-oriented work in progress. It was designed as a differentiated lightweight folded-plate structure that can be suspended between two masses of a building. The base geometrical plan layout is comprised of two nonconcentric arcs. The total arc length is approximately 100 meters (330 feet), and the span dimensions range from 7 to 16 meters (23 to 52 feet). In such classes of surface-active structures, the structural surfaces can be composed to form mechanisms that redirect forces. Therefore, structural continuity of the elements in two axes (surface resistance against compressive, tensile, and shear stresses) is the first prerequisite and first distinction of surface-active structures. Compression and tensile forces are measured as continuous force-flows across the whole length of the structure. These force-flows may differ to quite an extent depending on the way local or regional scale components are assembled.

Differentiation of the regularity of the structure must be carefully studied for its structural, as well as its geometric, implications. A physical origami-like structure maintains its triangular surface-area dimensions when translational and/or rotational operations are applied. Assuming the global geometry of the roof structure was nonuniform in nature, and given that the design required the differentiation of the folded-plate geometry according to structural load, the aim was to construct a digital parametric model that would mimic the behavior of the physical paper model and could be informed, beyond the geometrical logic of the system, by structural performance.

This folded-plate structure was modeled in Bentley's Generative-Components software, creating an environment that supported the adaptive exploration of the design solution. [Fig. 6] The local-scale component was composed of six plates connected to one common vertex; all surface areas of the elements were maintained constant when translational and rotational operations were applied. The global-scale model consisted of approximately four hundred plates and has, on the other hand, confirmed the doubt that when constrained to the global geometry restrictions posed by the two nonconcentric arcs, the plate surface dimensions will gradually change by a given increment across the longitudinal section of the roof.

Achim Menges is a partner in the Finnish firm Ocean North, a studio master at the Architectural Association in London, and director of the Institute for Computational Design at the University of Stuttgart, Germany.

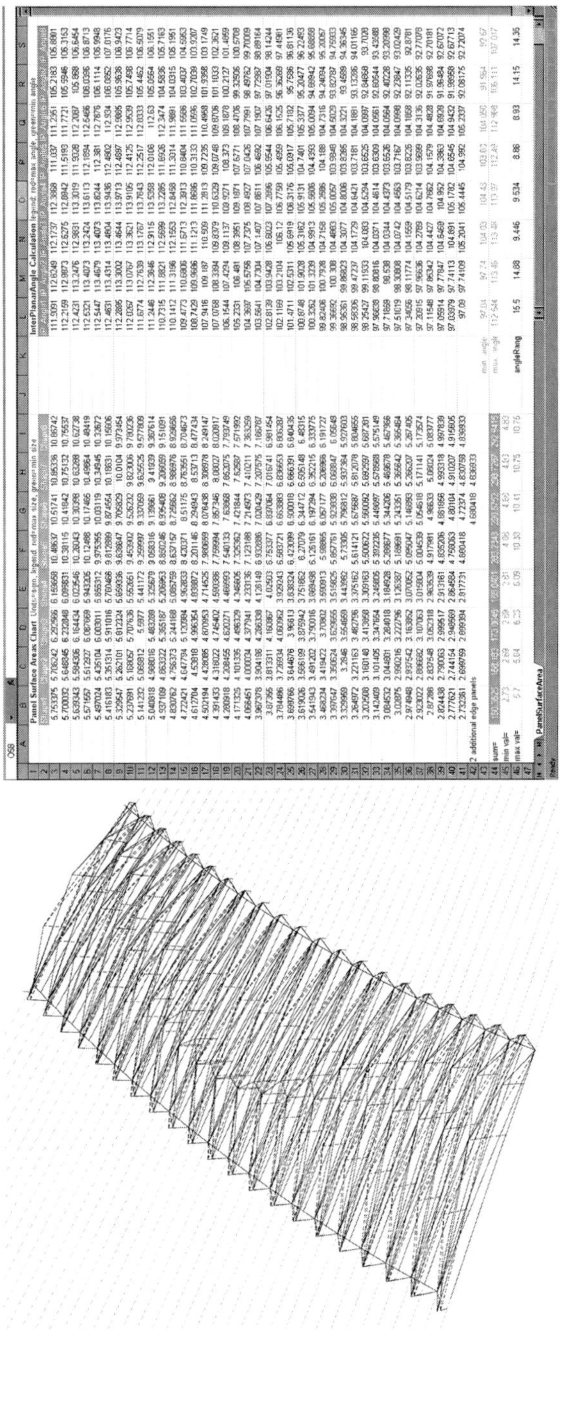

Fig. 6 / Parametric model of folded-plate roof project with spreadsheet of digitally derived geometric data, Lars Hesselgren and Neri Oxman, KPF London, 2005

USING BUILDING INFORMATION MODELING FOR PERFORMANCE- BASED DESIGN

Eddy Krygiel

Architect Eddy Krygiel outlines in this essay the well-known advantages of building information modeling (BIM) in creating project efficiencies, and provides case studies of how this technology is integrated with performance analysis tools to aid designers in creating more sustainable buildings. Illustrated with examples of new digitally enhanced processes, such as life-cycle cost/benefit analyses of design options and sophisticated daylighting simulation, Krygiel argues for the necessity of expanding opportunities for integrated design in architectural practice.

> A great building must begin with the immeasurable, must go through measurable means when it is being designed, and in the end must be immeasurable.
> —LOUIS KAHN

This quote by Louis Kahn describes architecture not as a product, but as an event and as a process. As designers, we do more than just create a building; we are tasked with trying to create an experience. The process of architectural design starts with the idea. This idea can be a concept or a simple napkin sketch. As we develop this idea, we iterate the concepts of space and form and how those spaces act and interact. We go through a scientific process of exploration through which we analyze, research, and investigate our designs with the ultimate goal to create more than just a building; we *want* to create an experience. Ultimately, the goal is to make the final experience one that will not only stand the test of time, but will also be environmentally responsible.

Creating a built experience within the architecture, engineering, and construction professions has become ever more challenging. Throughout the past one hundred years, the design and building industry has changed dramatically. Buildings have become much more complex with many more interrelated and integrated systems. During this period, we have added a number of new building systems and other layers of design. In the modern office building, for instance, we have added data and telecom services, air conditioning systems, security systems, sustainability goals, underground parking requirements, and enhanced building envelopes, among other features.

With this added complexity, architects, owners, and contractors have all had to adapt. These layers require more documentation from the architect to design the project, with significantly more sheets and details added to our drawing sets. More time is needed to coordinate all of these systems and to manage the additional supplies, trades, and installers on site for the contractor. And the owner's staff must now be more knowledgeable in order to maintain these systems over the life of the building. These and other factors have led to an overall decline in building performance and an increase in our overall energy consumption.

To review these factors in a bit more detail, it is necessary to get a wider picture of the design and construction industry over the past few decades by looking at historic industry trends for time, energy, and other resources in the last century. Assuming our methods do not change to adapt to the changing environment of design and construction, we may expect these trends to continue. While all industries have shown an overall increase in the use of materials during the twentieth century, the construction industry's consumption, which was fairly steady until the post–World War II era, has seen material use rise to more than five times that of all other industries combined.[1]

The construction labor costs are also increasing. The National Construction Employment Cost Index taken over a ten-year period from 1995 to 2005 shows increases in construction labor costs anywhere from 1.4 to 5.8 percent per quarter. Inflation, specialization, and building complexity are some of the reasons for these continual increases in costs.

These trends show that buildings are becoming more complicated to build. They require more resources to construct and operate, and this translates to the increasing life-cycle cost for a building. As these costs and complexities escalate, we are flooded with more information to manage about the building.

To keep up with the growing trends, we must find better ways to coordinate all of this information, clearly communicate it to the growing number of stakeholders involved, and better understand our role in the global ecology. By doing so, we can use the tools available to make our work more efficient by using the resources available to their maximum value. For this to happen, we will need to make a significant change in our process of design, interaction, and communication.

Our current model of team interaction works something like this: the design team begins by conceptualizing and drawing a project. After a certain point in the process, they will share documents with their consultants. This team will review and revise the drawings and share them back with the designers. Eventually, this package is passed to the contractor, who reviews the drawings and disseminates them to their subcontractors. These subcontractors redraw the drawings—in part—and pass them back to the contractor. The contractor will review them and pass them back to the architect who will pass them back to their consultants, who will review them, give them back to the architect, who will give them back to the contractor...and the cycle starts anew. This process is fraught with opportunities for displaced work and redundancy. Several opportunities exist for human error in copying and redrawing, not to mention a large loss in time simply sending information back and forth.

This style of workflow was possible and manageable when the amount of information changing hands was much smaller. As building

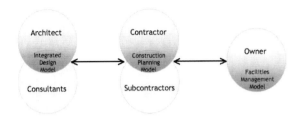

Fig. 1 / An integrated workflow, from *Green BIM*

complexity grows, it becomes harder and harder to manage the dramatic increase of information, team members, and documents within this system. [Fig. 1]

If we revisit our process and workflow using a more integrated approach, we can utilize BIM (building information modeling) as not only a documentation tool, but a medium of communication. BIM is a methodology of continual refinement, not one of drastic change. Success will occur by evolution, not revolution. BIM is defined as the creation and use of coordinated, consistent, computable information about a building project in design—parametric information used for design decision-making, production of high-quality construction documents, prediction of building performance, cost estimating and construction planning.

By sharing this model data back and forth with consultants, who are also using BIM, the system itself can track changes and coordinate the building design. This process of virtually building the building before the physical manifestation of the design becomes reality allows the teams to coordinate and error check at a much higher level. Elements of the design must interact as they do in reality. At a point, this model is shared with the contractor. They share the model with subcontractors who use the existing model and embellish the level of detail. This refinement still requires subcontractors to crosscheck a designer's work, but eliminates tedious redrawing. These additional, more detailed models are shared with the design team who can view this information referenced in their own model. This not only partially automates the review of these more complex systems, but also reduces the redundancy and human error prevalent in our current system. Once construction begins, the model is still referenced and kept up to date as site conditions are uncovered or modifications to the design are required. Once the project is complete, a virtualized, 3-D version of the building and all of its associated systems can be handed off to the owner for ongoing maintenance.

In order to embrace a change in our process, we need to adopt a substantially new manner of thinking. Not only is our current workflow in need of refinement, but we've recently become globally aware of the negative impacts our buildings have on the environment and the need to change our behaviors and designs. The sustainable movement within our profession has added additional layers and requirements to our work. Even for firms deeply rooted in "green" design, as owners and clients have become more educated in sustainability, we are increasingly required to provide metrics that measure the results of energy, daylight, and other strategies. This requirement for performance-based design reinforces the need to better manage and predict our designs.

Creating this change requires a shift in our culture and understanding. Adopting new tools at some level can be easy, but changing our established patterns and rethinking our habitual methods in our practice requires more diligence. This, however, is not outside our reach. There is a misconception within our industry that our steps as designers are simply designing and building.

The mainstream view of the architectural process is fairly basic. As anyone acquainted with the process of design is familiar, there is a lot more that goes into design. As designers, our steps are more accurately reflected by listening, researching, designing, building, occupying, and learning.

Each of these steps becomes important in the project life cycle. They can happen at the macro level where the entire project is idealized and constructed, or these same steps can help inform at a more micro level on a project with a particular building component or system.

This process is not linear but iterative. We do not complete these steps only once as designers but we will do them over and over again. We begin thinking about the client's and the building's needs well before putting pencil to paper. As we research ideas and materials, the design begins to take form. As this design unfolds, we explore prototyping, modeling, and experimenting with some of these ideas in a built form. We test (or occupy in the case of a finished building), then ideally learn from the results of this cycle and begin the cycle again. As we repeat this process with various building components and systems, eventually a design begins to take shape. Once it's complete, we can then learn from the various successes in that project to begin the next one. A successful project typically requires many iterations of these steps.

The extended benefits of BIM continue from conceptual design and documentation, through construction, and into building occupancy. As the use of BIM gains momentum, more and more of these ideas are becoming realized and able to be easily integrated into the design and construction process. The key advantages to a BIM-based workflow are integrated documents, design phase visualization, creation of a materials database, and incorporating sustainable strategies.

Integrated Documents

As all of the BIM drawings are placed within the single, integrated database or model, document coordination becomes relatively automatic. Because BIM is a database structure, the references are instantly coordinated after views are added to sheets in a drawing set. As buildings become increasingly complex, the number of sheets in a set of construction documents continues to grow. A building that might have once been documented with thirty or forty sheets fifty years ago can now take four times as many. Being able to automatically coordinate all of that information is no small feat and it can be time consuming to do it manually.

By integrating consultant information into the architectural drawings, we can derive additional benefits. Since the building is modeled in three dimensions, we can easily overlay architectural, structural, and mechanical models and check for interferences and conflicts within the building. Many BIM packages can also automate this process and provide reports of intersecting building components.

Fig. 2 / Design visualization of sunshading, from *Mastering Revit Architecture 2009*

Design Phase Visualization

Design phase visualization is another of the low-hanging fruits of BIM. Due to the 3-D nature of the model, we are able to almost instantly see the building from any angle, interior or exterior. This can be a great tool not only to aid in the design process of visualizing space, but also to convey ideas about the design to team members, clients, contractors, or regulatory agencies. Not only does this help with communication but, we can show the effects of the sun on the building during midday to help explain the importance of proper sunshading. [Fig.2]

Materials Database

Because BIM creates a database of the virtual building, assemblies (such as walls or roofs) that are modeled can be virtualized with their physical properties. When you add a wall in BIM, you are adding a 3⅝" metal stud between two layers of gypsum wallboard, or 7⅝" concrete masonry unit (CMU), or whatever else the wall is created out of in the design. Because the wall has a height and length, the database will allow you to create schedules of information about the wall or other objects within the model. You can quickly see how many linear feet or square feet of a given wall type you currently have in the design.

Sustainable Strategies

In the process of sustainable design, at one point during the design or documentation process, there comes a need to quantify the energy savings, the daylighting, or the recycled content in your building materials. This is done by using other applications to run analysis on the building design and deliver these metrics. In the days before BIM, this was done by remodeling the building in another application, typically one for each thing you wanted to measure. One model for energy, one for daylighting, and so on. This can not only be costly because of the time it takes but it is open to error, either through laboriously recreating the design intent of the design documents or from later design changes not getting added to the recreated model. With the use of BIM, we have the ability to take the building model geometry and move that directly into energy analysis or daylighting applications to calculate these metrics. This can help save time as well as eliminate geometric errors in the transition.

Energy Modeling

In the case of energy modeling and its relationship to BIM, there are three primary steps involved: modeling the building geometry, adding building loads, and performing the analysis.

If you compare the time it takes to perform each of these steps for the same building type across a variety of analysis packages, you will see very similar results. During years of integrated practice, I have found that more than 50 percent of the overall time needed to perform an energy analysis is consumed by modeling building geometry. This leaves 35 percent needed to add building loads followed by less than 15 percent to perform the actual analysis. By simply being able to reuse the model geometry and transfer the building design from BIM to the energy model, we can reduce the time needed to run an energy model by almost half.

The traditional process of energy modeling within our own office typically takes a couple weeks. Using the workflow established with BIM, we can now perform some types of energy analysis in half the time, do twice as many as before, or make energy analysis available to projects that would normally not have the fee to support the endeavor.

In my own practice, to demonstrate the basic use of energy analysis in building design, the design team compares two design options to understand what the relative energy impact is while also seeing the visual impacts those changes create. [Fig.3] On one project we chose to add a sunshading device to the west facade, but we wanted to see what the relative energy impact would be with this design change. We created two examples from the same BIM model and simply exported one

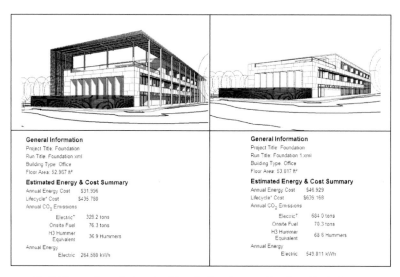

Fig. 3 / Comparison of a facade with and without sunshading, from *Mastering Revit Architecture 2009*

with the shading device on and the other with it turned off. In addition, we also wanted some metrics to figure out how improved the performance of one design would be over the other. To do this, we exported the design models to an energy analysis application, leveraging the ability to reuse the model geometry.

The annual energy performance for the building without the sunshade was $46,929. Because we were in an early stage of design and using this as a comparative calculation, we did not rely on the accuracy of that actual number. There are several factors that had not been taken into account during this particular analysis: building use cycle, building loads by equipment, thermal conductivity of the envelope, and so on. What we were studying was the relative effects of one design pitted against another. This comparison allowed us to qualify the design against the alternative: the building with the sunshade had an annual energy performance of $31,996 or an overall savings of 31 percent.

Daylighting

Streamlining the analysis process can also be extended to daylighting. Using a single model generated with BIM, we can analyze the same location in perspective within multiple applications. [**Fig. 4**]

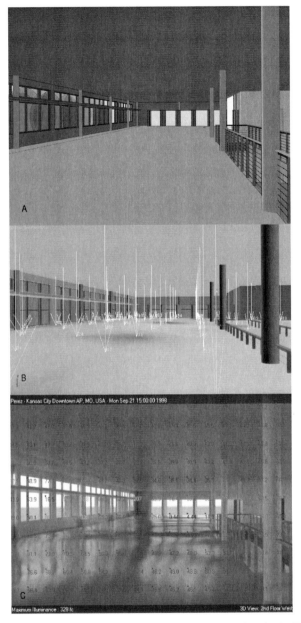

Fig. 4 / Three views from within the same model from the same location in different analysis programs. Top: building information model; middle: daylighting analysis model; bottom: visualization model; from *Mastering Revit Architecture 2009*

This reduces the time needed to complete the analysis from several weeks to only a day. Working in early stages of design, we can accurately quantify the amount of daylighting in a project and regularly test to see if we have hit certain daylighting design goals. If the project is pursuing Leadership in Energy and Environmental Design (LEED) accreditation, these same results can then be used for LEED credits 8.1 and 8.2 by switching from a perspectival view to a plan view. For these LEED credits, it's imperative to demonstrate a minimum lighting level within the building and access to views from all the acceptable spaces. This calculation, formerly very time consuming, can now be done very quickly. This also allows us to have better control over how much light we bring in. Depending on the building orientation, we might want to minimize fenestration so we can minimize heat gain. Daylighting tools allow us to optimize our light intake while not overreaching and thereby bringing in too much heat.

By eliminating the necessity to remodel geometry, we have not only improved the speed and accessibility of these types of analytical investigations but we have also improved the accuracy relative to the current state of the design. We are neither relying on the intuitive sense of the project designer to accurately depict the lighting or energy needs of the project nor are we relying on a secondary team member to interpret the drawings accurately and remodel the project in an analysis application. The same geometry that represents the current state of the design is being transferred from the design model to analysis almost instantly.

Recycled Materials

BIM by nature is a constantly up-to-date catalog of all the building material information that has been modeled. As we add walls, glazing, or any other element to the model, it is automatically added and tabulated. By leveraging this data, it becomes very easy to quickly calculate the amounts and volumes of these materials in the project. We can extend this to calculating the recycled content of the project as a whole or the content of any individual pieces. As an example, say we want to calculate the volume of fly ash in the building or the quantity of recycled steel. Many BIM applications have the ability to create dynamic schedules. These schedules can be created once in the course of the project and will continually maintain real-time information. In the case of our example, after we create the schedule in the BIM model, we can add building components to the model constructed of concrete (walls, columns, floors, and so on) and the sum of concrete and fly ash in the schedule will dynamically update. This gives the design team an accurate metric for the amount of recycled content in the project. This same type of schedule can then include any other materials in the project with recycled content.

Beyond energy modeling, daylighting, and calculating building materials, there are other sustainable strategies that can be taken advantage of when using BIM. All of these revolve around using the model to calculate areas and quantities of elements in the building design, such as rainwater harvesting (using roof areas in plan to size cisterns) and solar access (calculating orientation and roof area for solar panels).

The Future of BIM

In all of these advantages, the overall goal is to positively impact both the cost and schedule. BIM allows the design team the ability to optimize their workflow and to spend less time redrawing and more time designing. This allows more time to manage performance-based designs and sort through all of the complexities involved with today's modern building design and construction industry.

As BIM continues to evolve, direct analysis and comparative design strategies will be possible to view directly from the model. There are a number of the possibilities that are available today directly from BIM, but some of these require customizing existing applications to make their inclusion more seamless with the design process. [Fig.5]

The combined future of BIM and sustainability can help us move faster and more elegantly to a restored world and a healthy planet. There is no future, no next, if we do not change the ways in which we work, live, and play. Without overstating the connection between BIM and sustainable design, a few things are inevitable.

Parametric modeling will go well beyond mapping relationships between objects and assemblies. Both model and designer will have knowledge of climate and region. The model will know its building

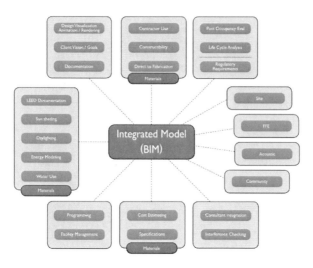

Fig. 5 / The future of BIM

type, insulation values, solar heat gain coefficients, and impact on the socioeconomic environment it resides within. It will inform the design team with regard to upstream impacts and downstream consequences of their choices.

As the building is modeled, prompts will inform the designer of the impact of the building orientation and envelope choices on the sizing of the mechanical system and comfort of its inhabitants. Projected rainfall and solar radiation calculations will be readily available to size cisterns and renewable energy systems. The future BIM will be a system completely interactive with key building information, climate information, user requirements, and triple bottom line impacts, so that design integration and data-return among all systems is immediate and symbiotic. Once the building is occupied, BIM will create an opportunity for a postoccupancy feedback loop.

If we choose to accept the ultimate design challenge—integration between nature and humankind, between the built and natural environments—we will need to rethink our attitude toward practice.

The relatively recent emergence of various models of integration suggests a promising convergence of thought in distinct yet related disciplines. We might now have the information and tools required to achieve integration in the technological sense, but what we must recover is our understanding of resource consumption, global regard for the environment, and social equity. With tools and wisdom intact, we can effectively work toward realignment with a sustainable planet, a restored planet, even a thriving planet. It is first and foremost a call to humanity to learn from nature—essentially a will to change.

Eddy Krygiel practices architecture in Kansas City, Missouri. He is a coauthor, with Brad Nies, of *Green BIM: Successful Sustainable Design with Building Information Modeling* and has coauthored numerous platform-specific instructional books.

Notes

Epigraph Louis Kahn quoted by/in John Lobell, *Between Silence and Light: Spirit in the Architecture of Louis I. Kahn* (Boston: Shambhala Publications, 1979).

1 Lorie A. Wagner, "Materials in the Economy—Material Flows, Scarcity, and the Environment," *U.S. Geological Survey Circular 1221*, U.S. Department of the Interior, U.S. Geological Survey, 2002.

INNOVATE OR PERISH:
NEW TECHNOLOGIES AND ARCHITECTURE'S FUTURE

David Celento

This polemical essay provides an economic and cultural critique of "business as usual" in architecture and illustrates with clear case studies a strong argument for the necessary adoption of new tools and methods. This article is a broad overview of new technologies and tools, and a compelling call for a "revolutionary" rather than "evolutionary" digital transformation of architectural practice. Key trends in contemporary practice are outlined, with examples ranging from mass-customized prefabricated building systems to ubiquitous computing.

Innovation is a development that people find useful or meaningful. To be innovative, architects—and works of architecture themselves—must become more responsive to their users and environments. In other words, they must incorporate feedback from their physical and cultural contexts rather than relying solely on conventional analytical or internal processes of development…from design to construction.

—ALI RAHIM, *Catalytic Formations*

While a few starchitects are being showered with praise, the forecast for many in the profession is partly to mostly cloudy. In 2005 only 2 percent of architects in Britain were "very happy" with their jobs—scoring at the bottom of thirty professions surveyed, and below civil servants.[1] These sentiments are hardly limited to Britain, as Dana Cuff illustrates in her *Architecture: The Story of Practice*.[2] Many among the general ranks of architecture are dismayed by the elusiveness of success and by their diminishing impact. There are two primary reasons for these phenomena—one cultural, the other methodological. Architects are among the very few providing *custom* design services in a product-infatuated society. This presents a profound problem, especially since few clients possess an understanding of the efforts necessary to create custom products, and even fewer are willing to adequately finance them. Second, while emerging digital technologies offer architects radically new possibilities for designing and building, current architectural speculation remains largely confined to timid *evolutionary* steps. Many in the profession are finding it difficult to leave behind the security blanket of past working traditions, while a few are simply choosing to pull it resolutely over their heads. Architects' refusal to embrace technological innovations invites their extinction. Less hidebound professions are ruthlessly shoving their way onto the turf once the sole domain of architects. The capabilities now provided by furniture system designers, sustainability consultants, construction managers, and engineers of all stripes have become so advanced that Martin Simpson of Arup suggests that architects may eventually become unnecessary—except, perhaps, as exterior stylists.[3]

To avoid obsolescence, architects need to increase demand for their skills by embracing emerging technologies that both stimulate and satiate consumer desires. For savvy architects with a dash of fortitude, *revolutionary* opportunities for creating enhanced predictability, complexity, branding, feedback, and economies of scale glimmer on the horizon. In this essay I will focus on the potentials of new design and building technologies, centering my comments on improving architecture's marketplace success. I invite speculation about the profound impact these technologies will have on designers' aesthetic, political, and social powers, which I will not address here.

The Case for Revolution

The *New Yorker*'s architecture critic Paul Goldberger is among those encouraging technological and business revolution, suggesting that, due to a rise in visual literacy and an insatiable quest for status among consumers, the time is ripe for architects to better harvest consumer desires. At the Fixed Income Forum in 2004 he noted, "I have to admit that the guy who drives a BMW or an Audi (whose parents drove an Oldsmobile) is not doing that only because he knows the Audi looks better—he is also doing it because of the status that ascribes to that name, and now, that status is available to (and sought by) a far broader segment of the population than it once was."[4] Why don't people lust after fine buildings to the extent that they do BMWs and Audis? The answer is simple: they can't. Architecture is sold in units of one. Architect-writers Dan Willis and Stephen Kieran and James Timberlake point toward technologies like building information modeling (BIM), mass customization, parametric design, and prefabrication as ways to pull architects out of their deepening ditch.[5] To this list we should add rapid prototyping, digital fabrication, ubiquitous computing, and online web ordering that permits product customization. What follows is a kind of *Rough Guide for the Intrepid Architect*—an insider's look at emerging technologies harboring both speculative possibilities and potential rocky shoals.

Tailor-made: Lessons from the Past

The question of whether to continue making "one-off" products or to make multiple variations of a product is one architects need to address. The saturation of manufactured goods today has had a profound impact not only on consumers, but also on providers of custom-made goods.

Consider the once flourishing tailoring trade, which, as a consequence of mass production, has shrunk to one sixteenth its size from 1920 to 1990.[6] Today, industrialized societies have gleefully traded fit, finish, and durability in exchange for savings, variation, brand-name identity, transient fashions, and immediate gratification. To imagine that this trend has little meaning for architects today would be foolhardy.

Michael Benedikt wrote:

> Architecture, as an industry, broadly conceived, has become less and less able to deliver a superior evolving and popularly engaging product that can compete with other more successful products.... And the less successfully architecture has competed with these diverse "growth industries," the less architects have been entrusted with time and money to perform work on a scale and with a quality that could perhaps turn things around.[7]

Today's consumers fundamentally lack an understanding of the complexity of creating *anything* tailor-made, let alone a substantive (and emotionally complex) object like a new building. Architectural clients soon find themselves lost amid a bewildering world of possibilities and complications that they are unprepared for because of their customary reliance on mass-produced goods. Rather than being exhilarated by the process, they are often left with remorse, since they must eliminate countless desirable options along the way.[8] While a few may enjoy the ambiguity, attention, cost, and complexity of the architectural process, many conditioned by the modern conveniences of ready-made products, web ordering, and overnight delivery are simply frustrated by it.

Rapid Prototyping Evolves to Rapid Fabrication

Would that client-related problems were architects' sole challenge. Because few innovations are specifically geared toward the construction industry, Toshiko Mori urges architects toward a practice model invigorated by "creative appropriation of advances made in non-architectural areas."[9] One such advance unnoticed by most architects (but celebrated by industrial designers, engineers, and manufacturers) is rapid prototyping technology—exciting for what it already is but deliriously enabling for where it will go. First introduced in 1986 by 3D Systems as stereolithography (SLA), this three-dimensional printer uses laser curing of resin, built one layer at a time, to create scale models.[10] SLA still thrives and has been joined by a number of other rapid prototyping devices that now include printing in plaster, plastics, rubber, resins, and even powdered metal that can be fused into durable parts by companies like Extrude Hone.[11] Once confined to volumes of less than one thousand cubic inches, these machines have grown within twenty years into wizards capable of printing full-size human figures.[12] Rapid *prototyping*—with weak modeling materials—is evolving into rapid *fabrication* of high-quality components used directly in medical implants, machinery parts, and aerospace applications. The rapid prototyping industry is burgeoning, with both scale and quality predicted to increase, while price declines.[13] In fact, the 3-D printing craze is just beginning, with Professor Hod Lipson of Cornell University launching an open-source project at Fabathome. org with instructions on how to build your own 3-D printer for $2,400, which can print in a variety of materials, including chocolate.[14]

As this trend continues, 3-D "printing" of full-scale building structures seems inevitable—especially considering that graduating digital designers are now creating 3-D models by printing them and are eager to realize large-scale fabrication of complex forms that can't readily be built by hand. Large 3-D-printed structures (up to 14 feet by 20 feet by 8 feet) can already be made in concrete using a prototype unit developed by University of Southern California industrial engineer Behrokh Khoshnevis. Khoshnevis can see no reason why rapid prototyping technology won't eventually be scaled up, especially as material costs come down and funding increases.[15] [Fig. 1] Architects using rapid fabrication technology at a building scale could economically create complex singular designs as well as customizable multiples. First these will appear as building components and later as full-scale structures. In 1957, a Massachusetts Institute of Technolory (MIT) collective envisioned the plastic Monsanto House of the Future for Disneyland.[16] If fifty years later houses of the future were envisioned as daringly, they would surely be the offspring of a union between digital design and automated rapid fabrication. Not limited to simplistic adobe-esque load-bearing styles, these houses would come in a variety

Fig. 1 / Prototyping for 3-D printing of structural forms in real
construction materials

of forms ranging from traditional to avant-garde and would be available in many durable colors, textures, materials, and translucencies. Complete with injury-free, pliable children's rooms, these structures (likely constructed with five-axis extrusion heads and sonic welding already used for utility piping) will be capable of complex shapes that would make even Antoni Gaudí envious. A significant side effect will be that ornament will again proliferate, since complexity will no longer have a direct relationship to labor cost. Such structures would replace traditional stick-framing and allow a variety of traditional forms and materials to continue, but could also be fully exploited by modernists interested in displaying the intrinsic nature of these monolithic materials. Structures printed in multiple materials could integrate expensive nuisance items like mechanical chases, extruded plumbing channels, and conduits complete with electricity-conductive slurries. Integrating features like showers, sinks, shelving, cabinets, furniture, and far more would eliminate much of the current time-consuming coordination between various trades. Electrical power could be fashioned like circuit boards with plug-and-play wiring harnesses like in computers or cars, serving as a nervelike web running just below the building's skin, eliminating traditional outlets and permitting power almost anywhere.

Environmentalists will rejoice over printed buildings, since 92 percent of building waste is now the result of renovation and demolition.[17] Dramatic reductions would be possible because "printed" structures would be almost entirely recyclable, since the diverse materials used would easily be disassembled and auto-sorted much the way trash is today. Additionally, designers will be able to easily perform analysis of finite structural elements, enabling a whole new level of structural comprehension and daring, and wresting a good deal of power from structural engineers. Best of all for consumers, the duration, amount of material, and cost of a project will be fairly precisely known in advance. Of course, the inevitable curve ball hurled at architects is if (read: *when*) people themselves design and build their "dream houses" using software programs like Google's free 3-D modeler SketchUp in conjunction with intrepid 3-D-printing contractors, thus ensuring lively design review hearings for some time to come.

Parametric Design

Because parametric design is ideally suited to the mastery of rapid fabrication, John Nastasi of the Product-Architecture Lab at the Stevens Institute of Technology believes that parametric design skills need to be among the dozen or so capabilities that define the digital toolboxes of forward-looking architects.[18] Parametric design allows users to modify relationships between various features while tracking the history of those changes, thus updating all interrelationships performed after the modification. A very simple example of this might be a hole in a wall that will always be automatically placed at one half the height of the wall, regardless of the wall's size.[19] This is a common technique used in product fabrication, but the precision involved in

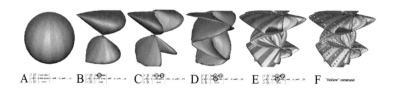

A   B   C   D   E   F

Fig. 2 / Parametric design in six easy steps/minutes, using Grapher by Apple, 2007 manufacturing software (accurate to thousandths of an inch) can be limiting to free architectural design exploration. Thus several architects like Greg Lynn, Office dA, and Pennsylvania State's Graduate Design Research Studio's director Ali Rahim have instead adopted the animation program Maya because it permits more fluid design exploration with less emphasis on manufacturing tolerances. Maya has several beneficial attributes that aid in conceptual design studies: manipulation of mathematical algorithms using embedded language scripting can autogenerate forms as complex as skyscrapers (commonly done by students of Kostas Terzidis at the Harvard Graduate School of Design [GSD]), ease rapid prototyping of study models, and create compelling and informative walk-through animations.[20] The number of potential parametric relationships is limited only by the diversity of data and the imagination of the designer. The benefit for architects is that a fully developed singular parametric design project may be easily tweaked to create wildly dissimilar results for other projects. Complex results dazzle the uninitiated, but can be surprisingly simple to generate for those with an understanding of how parametric design works. [Fig.2]

BIM

Parametric design goes well beyond mere formal pyrotechnics. Inherent to BIM is parametric design software tied to data contained in spreadsheets. Changes made to either the digital model or the database automatically update and coordinate throughout the model and spreadsheet.[21] Due to the extent of the previsualization it allows prior to construction, BIM diminishes ambiguity, reduces errors, and generates savings for clients.[22] The American Institute of Architects (AIA), through its Technology in Architectural Practice committee, even has a special awards program for BIM projects.[23] In theory, since architects deal with ever-changing information, BIM sounds almost too good to be true. In practice, benefits will not be realized without some possibly serious drawbacks that I will soon discuss.

Vladimir Bazjanac, at the Lawrence Berkeley National Laboratory, marvels at the uniqueness of the current architectural process, commenting that architecture, without sophisticated previsualization provided by BIM, is little more than a "*convince-*

build-pray modus operandi."[24] Bazjanac sees BIM as a way for architects to emulate manufacturers' efforts to imbue project delivery with greater certainty. He is partially right, but what he is perhaps missing is that, in the world of products, complete documentation of minutiae makes economic sense only because design is a very small fraction of the total cost of products. This is not the case with architecture. Chris Kasabach, director of product marketing for BodyMedia (the Cooper-Hewitt's biomedical darling), indicates that because of digital design models, industrial designers are changing their processes and teaming up with fabricators early in the design phase.[25] The result is that during the prototyping phase an increasing amount of digital redesign is being done remotely by fabricators. When asked who pays for this redesign, Kasabach enthusiastically responds, "The prototyping companies do. Essentially, they consider 'design' an insignificant and necessary cost of manufacturing."[26] Despite the disparity between products and architecture, the General Services Administration (GSA) has required architects to perform full BIM modeling on selected projects since 2003 and is now requiring partial BIM models on *all* federally funded projects, and is considering full BIM for all future projects.[27] Their experience is a reduction in change orders saving the GSA up to 10 percent of total construction costs.[28] Clearly clients are benefiting, but what about architects? When I questioned Luciana Burdi, head of Capital Asset Management for the State of Massachusetts, on the lack of increased architectural fees for BIM projects, she replied, "Architects are paid to provide buildings without errors, why should they be paid *more* to do this?" For clients, BIM infatuation is easy to understand—they want savings, and the rigorous BIM process complies.

Unfortunately, this magic elixir has one possibly terminal side effect for architects—clients are developing an insatiable expectation for perfection from uniquely made buildings. While BIM possesses fairly powerful tools for error *reduction*, it is simply incapable of error *elimination*. Burdi went on to express frustration over an expensive error in a recent BIM project—one that she felt should have been caught by the architect prior to construction—thus underscoring that for architects there is a distinct danger that BIM will result in a triple-whammy: more work, less profit, and increased liability. Despite these challenges, 34 percent of architects are using some form of BIM modeling. But for most this is only during conceptual stages to generate rudimentary cost data and quantity takeoffs helpful in evaluating the expense impacts of various schematic designs—not for full BIM production.[29] Profitable implementation of full BIM seems to require at least one of two components. The first is for architects to retain ownership of BIM data so that they may use that data in future projects of similar typologies to amortize the first use-costs of development. However, the GSA prohibits this and wants sole ownership of the data. The second, using the industrial design model, is for architects to bring fabricators with BIM skills into the design process early for assistance in the development of the digital BIM model. This, too, is prohibited by the GSA since they require traditional design-bid-build process. Ostensibly the group with the most lobbying power for beneficial BIM conditions for architects is the AIA TAP committee. Stephen Hagan, director of the GSA's Project Knowledge Center, has served on this committee for the past four years and was chair last year.[30] When I asked Douglas Paul, AIA director of professional practice, whether this relationship might not be an overly cozy one for the GSA at the possible expense of architects' well-being, Paul indicated that this concern had never been raised before.[31] Hagan seems a good fellow and has earned Fellow of the American Institute of Architects (FAIA) wings, but if I'm the first to question—make that be *astounded by*—this relationship, one can only wonder who is spiking the AIA's water cooler. The power of BIM is well documented, and its software will continue to improve. However, full BIM modeling for singular enterprises is ultimately not beneficial for architects, since the time (and thus, cost) of such a complex endeavor is much higher than normal one-off design services. Development of a full BIM model is almost as complex as physically making the actual object and one that makes economic sense only in a mass-production/customization context. Alternatively, one could also be paid very handsomely for singular full BIM modeling—but this seems unlikely. An imperfect but illustrative parallel in manufacturing would be if Boeing were contacted to digitally design and construct a one-of-a-kind "blue-sky" airplane. The client is interested in exclusive rights to Boeing's five years worth of design data, prohibits Boeing from making more than one plane, will only pay for error-free parts, and expects to pay little (or no) more than the cost of a standard plane of similar size.[32] Boeing wouldn't even bother to return the call, yet architects are competing for design opportunities where the conditions aren't that much different.

The Digital Master Builder

> Lacking at the start of the twentieth century was the information needed to effect real change in the way we build. Tools to represent and transfer information instantly and completely are with us today. They allow connections among research, design, depiction, and making that have not existed since specialization began during the Renaissance.
>
> —STEPHEN KIERAN AND JAMES TIMBERLAKE,
>   *Refabricating Architecture*

Once, as "master builders," architects both designed and built structures. However, architects relinquished their direct role in the building process centuries ago and have instead relied on 2-D drawings to describe their visions to specialized builders. Today this communication process is rapidly changing as a direct result of digital fabrication introduced in 1971 by technology developed at the French automotive company, Renault.[33] Drawings are being augmented—if not entirely replaced—by processes that permit 3-D fabrication of complex forms directly from architects' data. In this context, the much-vaunted Guggenheim Museum Bilbao (1997), celebrated for its convoluted artful forms, is far more groundbreaking for its use of innovative digital construction processes in which Gehry's office assumed responsibility for the accuracy of fabrication.[34]

Although this is not in itself news, direct digital communication has reinvigorated the concept of master builder for a few architects. Repopularized some thirty years ago by the radical Jersey Devil architectural group, the design-build method means the responsibility for design and production are provided by the same party. Pedagogically significant since it opens up a fertile dialectic between design and tectonics, there is again tremendous interest in this model in academia—most notably in the revered Rural Studio, initiated in 1993 at Auburn University by the late Samuel Mockbee. Many other schools have

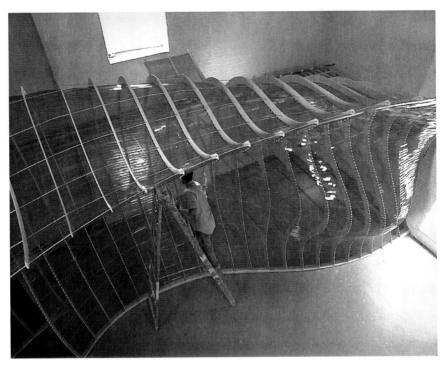

Fig.3 / Installation, Internet Radio Station, William Massie Studio, P.S.1,
Cranbrook Academy of Art, Bloomfield Hills, Michigan, 2006

adopted design-build in their curriculum, often relying on digital fabrication for components in such things as Solar Decathlon projects, material research, formal investigations, and community-based initiatives.[35] The upshot of this is that more emerging practitioners are once again enthusiastic about possibilities inherent in varying levels of participation in the actual *making* of design. Design-build today has two distinctly different branches—the decidedly larger one (dominated by contractors) deals primarily with *profit* optimization, while the smaller (but more interesting tectonically) deals with *product* optimization. A few architectural firms have thrown themselves into the opportunities presented by this latter area by exploring the union of 3-D design with 3-D fabrication, creating works that range from sculptural objects and surfaces to full-sized buildings. These provocative offerings (often exploiting the possibilities of parametric design) are from the likes of William Massie, Thom Faulders, Forsythe + MacAllen, Evan Douglis, SHoP Architects, John Nastasi, Byoung Soo Cho, and many others.[36] [Fig. 3] The attention that these efforts are receiving suggests that design-build innovation can readily yield increased stature for talented newcomers. Further reason that architects should pay more attention to this area is that at the current rate of change in the building industry, design-build project delivery is expected to surpass traditional design-bid-build methods by 2010.[37] For architects with the courage to branch out from their well-entrenched methodologies, tremendous opportunities for increased complexity, control, and economies of scale through digital fabrication lie ahead. Such endeavors permit industrious architects to focus design efforts and material explorations on specific areas of architectural significance (regardless of scale) and thus reassert themselves as master builders.

Prefabrication

As was outlined in a report by the British Department of Trade and Industry, the advantages of building houses in factories abound—reductions in time for site work, weather disruptions, coordination of workers, delivery, labor shortages, waste, damage in shipping, and water and energy use, plus increases in recycling, precision, and quality control. Collectively these benefits generate a dramatic reduction in total embodied energy and environmental impact of structures, despite the cost of shipping the finished product.[38] Prefabricated housing (including "mobile homes") is a $54 billion industry in which the United States provides 80 percent of the stock globally. The United States leads sales, with 6.4 percent of its population living in prefabricated units, followed by Japan, and with Latin America the fastest growing market.[39] Ninety-seven percent of manufactured houses move only once from factory to site.[40] While possibly energy-efficient and well-made, prefabricated houses have struggled to gain cultural acceptance in the United States due to the lingering dread associated with sagging mobile homes propped up on blocks with wheels dangling like vestigial organs—an unexpected result of tax and zoning laws. Convincing antidotes for this unsavory image have been presented in delightful neomodernist efforts presented by *Dwell*

magazine and by over thirty designers at Fabprefab.com—many of
whom address possibilities of prefabrication decoupled from a static
foundation. Why has prefabrication failed to catch on? My sense is
that several components are missing from current efforts, and a few
large hurdles remain to be cleared. The obstacles come in the form of
close-minded community groups, outdated zoning codes, cainopho-
bic design review boards, and restrictive covenants. These fears stem
from a stigmatization of the typology that arose as a result of the post–
World War II housing boom when prefabrication (think Levittown)
meant "cheap" in both economic and cultural senses. By contrast,
Sears's houses prior to World War II were neither, selling seventy-
five thousand units from 1908 through 1940, many of which bear historic plaques today.[41] Within Sears's treasured antique catalogs are
salient clues for future efforts—the creation and promotion of desire,
industrial commitment large enough so that results are not simply
regional, and tight integration of diverse systems. KieranTimberlake
has soundly scored on many of these counts with their Loblolly House
built by Bensonwood Homes, to be offered in a production format
by LivingHomes, an environmentally focused prefabricator. Steven
Glenn, founder of LivingHomes, notes, "If our major focus is making the product better, quicker, cheaper, and with a smaller ecologi-
cal footprint, we need a high level of technology integration."[42] What
follows is a paradigm-shifting vision for dwellings. For the adventur-
ous, the recreational vehicle (RV) offers an often overlooked alternative form of prefabrication. Travel trailers (RVs without engines) were
once so popular that in 1935, the predictor of the stock market crash,
Roger Babson, hazarded another shocker, "Within twenty years, more
than half of the population of the United States will be living in automobile trailers."[43] Indeed, prior to World War II, there were over four
hundred manufacturers of travel trailers, yet Babson's power of prog-
nostication failed to identify the war that quickly gutted the industry.[44]
Today, with baby boomers eagerly embracing alternative retirement
lifestyles, tremendous growth is once again occurring in the market for
mobile dwellings. A University of Michigan study indicates that one
in twelve vehicle owners currently possesses an RV, and one in six surveyed intends to buy an RV within five years.[45] For increasing numbers,
RVs have become a desirable form of temporary or permanent living

Fig. 4 / Rendering, Breckenridge Perfect Cottage, Christopher Deam, Breckenridge, Colorado, 2006

Fig. 5 / PRO/con Package Homes Tower, Jones, Partners: Architecture, 2000

reinvigorated by wireless voice and data technology, easy financing (complete with second-house tax benefits), significant configurability, integration of premium technologies for home theater, advanced energy management, integration of green elements like biodiesel fuel and solar electricity generation, and, perhaps most appealing, "drop-of-the-hat" mobility surrounded by one's "stuff."

The design of mobile dwellings represents a significant opportunity not being taken by architects, with the exception of Christopher Deam in his work for Breckenridge and Airstream.[46] [Fig. 4] Architects could and should be pushing the boundary of RVs in the form of technologically enabled customizable structures with interchangeable components that would permit a variety of shipping techniques over land and sea. And with some ingenuity, the results need not look anything like the lumbering behemoths squatting near highway exit ramps. Mobile dwellings have something else going for them. With enough shipping containers now in existence to wrap around the equator—stacked two high—inventive dwellings made from these modules makes some sense from a purely economic point of view.[47] Work by Wes Jones of Jones, Partners: Architecture, Los Angeles; Jennifer Siegal of Office for Mobile Design, Los Angeles; Hybrid Design of San Francisco; LOT-EK of New York City; Quik House designer Adam Kalkin of Bernardsville, New Jersey; and others has inventively explored the prefabricated shipping container as a base module for houses. [Fig. 5] While these projects may have the ripped-designer-jeans crowd worked up into a lather, their raw industrial quality will ultimately hinder wide public acceptance. However, they do offer an estimable lesson to carry forward: a standardized chassis using existing globally integrated transportation techniques. Mobile products based on such a chassis would allow multiple designers to create products that could easily work together to permit mass customization in a way portentously touted twelve years ago by B. Joseph Pine II, author of the groundbreaking book *Mass Customization*.[48] Like the prefabricated living suites by Piikkio Works for the cruise ship industry, these creations need not look at all like shipping containers.[49] Storing increasing numbers of RVs is not a trivial problem. Rather than being parked in rural driveways or at sprawling storage facilities and camp sites (as is done with most RVs today), these dwellings could be lived in daily and driven, towed, lifted, stacked, and slotted into a variety of attractive rural, suburban, or urban structures and thus partially supplant vacation cottages, rental apartments, condos, and college dorms. They could be cleverly integrated into well-disguised slots in houses and high rises, or displayed in full "messy vitality" depending upon their context. Today, with almost one third of the U.S. population renting their dwellings, architects pursuing this new typology might increase home ownership for low-income people.[50] Imagine giving your newborns their own chassis at birth—their first house, something they could take with them when they leave the nest, replacing at least a decade of apartment rentals with minimal "docking fees" as they educate themselves, move about, and develop their careers. This concept (which I call a *Jump Box*) offers technologically sophisticated, compact, and amenity-rich living. Well-branded models will be featured in magazines and become as desirable as cars—with one big difference: a durable chassis would permit every aspect to be easily upgraded over time as fashions, finances, and technology evolve. With one in six U.S. dwellers moving every year, relocaters would be liberated from the complex and expensive affair involved in renting (or buying) a new abode, then frantically packing and unpacking for the next several months—a process equal in stress to the loss of a loved one or divorce.[51]

Instead, a spicy little structure could be ready to ship to a new location in an hour or less, consuming a fraction of the energy required to move into (and live out of) a bloated McMansion. Architects should be pioneering the design of these enabling, productlike dwellings along with an expansive range of ever-evolving components. Architects could also provide the vision necessary for a whole new typology of dynamic "docking" structures beneficially integrated into the urban context. We now see an explosive growth of rural-bound RVs, partially since cities are simply incapable of accommodating them. Cities that embrace mobile structures would certainly benefit on many levels from an influx of the highly desirable, increasingly mobile "creative class," while reducing commuter congestion and increasing tax revenue.[52]

Ubiquitous Computing

Mark Weiser, the recognized father of embedded technology, wrote, "The most profound technologies are those that disappear. They weave themselves into the fabric of everyday life until they are indistinguishable from it."[53] Accordingly, intelligent architectures, with the ability to recognize and incorporate sophisticated sensors already inherent in cell phones, clothing, and other products would permit powerful feedback loops about their users, thus improving the design and usefulness of environments. With origins in 1946 Soviet spy devices, various forms of ubiquitous computing—embedding computation into the environment and everyday objects—today appear in such amenities as the E-ZPass, cardswipe doors, automated parking systems, and tracking of library books.[54] Radio frequency identification (RFID) tags (small radio receiving chips) enable this technology. In accordance with the idea outlined a decade ago by Christian W. Thomsen in *Visionary Architecture*, a short list for architects of the possibilities enabled by RFID technology includes such things as signage displayed legibly in one's own language, doors unlocking as one simply walks up to them, lighting and sound adjusting to suit one's preferences or mood, blinds cooperating with heating and cooling cycles, auto-sorting of waste, rooms that could auto-adjust to optimize performance based on the number of occupants, and coffee makers that would leap into action when you wake up.[55]

Branding Desire

These emerging technologies with implications for architecture include some necessary ingredients—but require a generous dollop of desire. According to a recent article by business professor Banwari Mittal, our culture relies heavily upon brand-name products for self-identity, and membership in today's consumer collective is gained through the purchase of celebrated popular products rather than unique hand-knitted sweaters from Grandma.[56] Oxymoronically, people assert their "individuality" through their display of mass brands and accessories. Accordingly, one begins to understand the challenges for modernist architecture as outlined in Anthony Alofsin's *The Struggle for Modernism*—deviation from commonly accepted architectural practices is for visionaries, heretics, and hippies, not ordinary consumers.[57] As Michael Sorkin suggested in his pungent *Harvard Design Magazine* article "Brand Aid," "to create the success of any commercial multiple, the brand is critical.... And, of course, celebrity is the main measure of authority in Brandworld."[58] With several starchitects already on the lips of today's consumers (Rem Koolhaas, Frank Gehry, Zaha Hadid, Michael Graves, Philippe Starck...) fame may be enough to generate desire—but only if your name is *already* a brand. Peggy Deamer weighs in on the topic of fame versus brand:

> [Architecture] does not conform easily to what we have said characterizes fame (inaccessibility and the clear identification of author with product). Likewise, its size, expense, and long production time make each object unique and singular, precluding it from notions of branding (repeatability and accessibility). It is perhaps for this reason that *fame* and *branding* are both elusive in architecture.[59]

Yet Deamer seems to waffle about the importance of brand, squeezing off a potshot at brand-makers, "Fame is still linked to creativity, while branding is linked only to calculation."[60] Mass-produced products gain popularity and fame for reasons that go well beyond simple branding, including ostensibly stolid ones: reputation, value, desire, durability, and performance. Branding is not the destination but simply the vehicle that propels products into the limelight. To wit, and perhaps contrary to Deamer's assertion, oxo Good Grips have not garnered over ninety awards simply because their name is a calculated palindrome.[61]

True, brand manufacturers enjoy the ability to chart *quantitatively* the sizzle in their steak through market share statistics. Conversely, architects seem to rely more upon an ethereal drool index based on abstract *qualitative* data, like published work, who is invited to serve on what jury, the number and type of awards received, and intangible associations with glitterati including the usual heavy-hitting patrons, critics, notables, and fat cats. Do these divergent methods suggest a *lack of creativity* for manufacturers or a *lack of reality* for architects? Architects who seek wider success may need to brand their work in recognizable ways. Instead of trying to launch a brand from a position

Fig. 6 / Rendering of aerial view, Resi/Rise Skyscraper, KOL/MAC Studio,
New York, 1999

of obscurity, architects might associate with recognized brand names as Michael Graves did in partnering with Lindal Cedar Homes and Target to offer customizable pavilion structures through Target's website.[62] The one formidable aspect, as in dating, is that such partnering requires give as well as take.

Accessorizing Desire

Architects now operate under the false premise that people *want* to be involved in the creation of their buildings. This supercilious belief flatters architects' need to be needed, but is simply not borne out in practice. People love to accessorize, and nothing does this better than the World Wide Web. Online ordering represents a powerful opportunity for architects because of its multilayered ability to tender interaction, option visualization, pricing variations, data linking, and statistical analysis of items that generate consumer interest—thus providing a beneficial feedback loop for product development—as is now being done by Bensonwood Homes with their online building configurator.[63] Of further attraction to architects is that virtual 3-D models are often all that needs to be displayed, and the virtual revels in this task. A stunning example of a saturated online experience worth emulating may be found at MINIUSA.com, where we can fantasize about our new individualized MINI Cooper that (BMW swears) can be built in over ten million configurations. These include tasty options like sports suspension, Bang and Olufsen stereo, and of course, racing stripes—complete with a running total of the price and the ability to save your order for future fidgets. Architects harnessing this process could interact with consumers to customize their fantasies in a way that *both* find rewarding. A provocative conceptual poke in this direction may be seen in the Resi/Rise Skyscraper (1999, unbuilt) by KOL / MAC Studio, exhibited at the 2004 Venice Biennale International Exhibition, complete with a configurable online ordering system. [Fig.6]

A Peek at the Future

John Habraken, theoretician and former head of architecture at MIT, suggested at the 2007 conference Global Place: Practice, Politics, and the Polis that "modernism was in essence an age of transition. Architecture needs to be well informed and restless, offering advanced personal environments."[64] Even the venerable Frei Otto expresses concern for the current architectural climate, writing, "Today's architecture is at a turning point. The big trends of the last decade are outlived and only a few buildings in the world manifest architectural perfection while paving new ways into the future."[65] These warnings, considered in light of the dramatic and unprecedented changes which our society is rapidly undergoing, suggests we are reaching a tipping point toward new architectures. Architects are teetering on this tipping point. The current architectural model is unduly weighed down by centuries of outdated working methodologies and singular prototype creation. Three primary limitations must be quickly dealt with. First, the absence of substantive feedback loops (loops evident in product-design but absent in architecture) prohibits in-depth analysis, adaptation, and evolution of our work. Second, a lack of economies of scale because of one-off production prohibits architects from fully integrating new technologies. Third, consumers' desire for an architecture that evokes status and collective identity is not well-served by the one-off, brand-free model of most architecture. Despite architects' fear of global homogeneity, people's expectations for all products (yes, including architecture) have been dramatically reshaped in the last decade by increasingly positive experiences with web ordering processes that suit their needs and lifestyles. As a result, a desire is growing among consumers for architectural alternatives that go well beyond architecturally erotic, postrationalized digital forms, moving architecture into a realm that Ali Rahim suggests is "useful, meaningful, and sustaining."[66] To increase its desirability and market share, architectures need to harness emerging technologies and tap more deeply into consumer desires, using both plurality and branding in product delivery methods. These efforts would be self-correcting—they provide an opportunity for architects to evaluate the success of their offspring quantitatively. Doing so would also encourage architects to move beyond "isms" geared toward revolutionizing aesthetic and social agendas every decade or so—a phenomenon that architects themselves can't even keep up with—let alone the public at large, since architectural journals which feature these sorts of rapid-fire volleys (including this one) are rarely found nestled between the *Economist* and *Vanity Fair* at newsstands. Two decades of fanciful catalogs stuffed in mailboxes have done more to shape popular taste (and educate people about design) than the club of architectural priests that has elevated its game by preaching to the converted while leaving out the laypeople that architects ultimately need. There are manifold implications inherent in these musings that are beyond the scope of this essay; I will leave the morality plays for others. What appears certain is that enhanced business success for architects will depend on weaving the technologies explored here into the making of more desirable and functional environments for an evolving populace experiencing tremendous technological, cultural, and environmental change. Who is better suited for this task than those who envision futures and coordinate innumerable specialists already? For architects, embracing these possibilities is on the one hand frighteningly simple and on the other hand scandalously improbable, for it involves nothing more than the abandonment of thousands of years of precedent.

David Celento is an architect and assistant professor of architecture and digital fabrication at Pennsylvania State University.

Notes

Epigraph 1 Ali Rahim, *Catalytic Formations: Architecture and Digital Design* (New York: Taylor & Francis, 2006), 3.

Epigraph 2 Stephen Kieran and James Timberlake, *Refabricating Architecture: How Manufacturing Methodologies Are Poised to Transform Building Construction* (New York: McGraw-Hill, 2003), 23.

1 City and Guilds Institute, "Happiness Index Survey," London, http://www.city-and-guilds.co.uk/cps/rde/xchg/SID-0AC0478C-4B086A92/cgonline/hs.xsl/2342.html (accessed January 2007).

2 Dana Cuff, *Architecture: The Story of Practice* (Cambridge, MA: MIT Press, 1991).

3 Martin Simpson, visiting lecturer in Harvard University Graduate School of Design "CadCam2" course of professor Daniel Schodek, April 10, 2006.

4 Paul Goldberger, "Does Architecture Matter? Thoughts on Buildings, Design, and the Quality of Life," Fixed Income Forum, Chicago, March 25, 2004, http://www.paulgoldberger.com/speeches.php?speech=doesarchitecturematter#articlestart.

5 Dan Willis and Todd Woodward, "Diminishing Difficulty: Mass Customization and the Digital Production of Architecture," *Harvard Design Magazine*, Fall/Winter 2006; Stephen Kieran and James Timberlake, *Refabricating Architecture: How Manufacturing Methodologies are Poised to Transform Building Construction* (New York: McGraw-Hill, 2003).

6 Joel Garreau, "America, Minus a Human Factor: From Guns to Bunions, a Statistical Portrait that Doesn't Quite Add Up," *Washington Post*, April 26, 2006, C01.

7 Michael Benedikt, "Less for Less Yet," *Harvard Design Magazine*, Winter/Spring 1999, 11.

8 Ziv Carmon, Klaus Wertenbroch, and Marcel Zeelenberg, "Option Attachment: When Deliberating Makes Choosing Feel Like Losing," *Journal of Consumer Research* 30, no. 1 (June 2003): 15–29.

9 Toshiko Mori, *Immaterial / Ultramaterial: Architecture, Design, and Materials* (Cambridge, MA: Harvard Design School in association with George Braziller, 2002), xvii.

10 Inventor: Charles W. Hull; Assignee: UVP, Inc; Patent number: 4575330; Filing date: Aug. 8, 1984; Issue date: March 11, 1986.

11 Fused deposition modeling (FDM) prints molten plastics in fine layers. Selective laser sintering (SLS) uses powdered plastics and metals that are cured by laser. ZCorp, a Massachusetts Institute of Technology invention, uses standard inkjet heads printing colored adhesive into a descending bed of a gypsum or rubberized powder and PolyJet, which lays down microfine layers of plastics or rubber resins that are rapidly cured by ultra-violet light in a fashion so fine that even four-point text is legible.

12 Materialise, Mammoth SLA, 2100mm x 650mm x 780mm, 2006, http://www.materialise.com/prototypingsolutions/stereo_ENG.html (accessed January 2007).

13 Wohlers Associates, *Wohlers Report 2006*, http://www.wohlersassociates.com/2006info.htm.

14 Tom Simonite, "Desktop fabricator may kick-start home revolution," NewScientist, http://fabathome.org/wiki/uploads/1/14/NewScientistTech1-9-2007.pdf; Fab@Home, "Main Page," http://www.fabathome.org/wiki/index.php?title=Main_Page.

15 Behrokh Khoshnevis, interview with the author, December 19, 2006.

16 Peter Hall, "Living for Tomorrow," *Metropolis*, December 2002, http://www.metropolismag.com/html/content_1202/mit/index.html.

17 Franklin Associates, "Characterization of Building-Related Construction and Demolition Debris in the United States," Report No. EPA530-R-98-010, The U.S. Environmental Protection Agency Municipal and Industrial Solid Waste Division Office of Solid Waste, 1998, 2–11, Table 8.

18 John Nastasi, in a lecture in the Harvard University Graduate School of Design "CadCam2" course taught by professor Daniel Schodek, April 3, 2006.

19 According to a 2004 Wohlers Associates survey with J. Greco, the leading programs in order of use by industry are Pro/ENGINEER, CATIA, Unigraphics, Mechanical Desktop, Inventor, SolidWorks, and Solid Edge, http://wohlersassociates.com/2004contents.html.

20 Kostas Terzidis, *Algorithmic Architecture* (Boston: Architectural Press, 2006).

21 International ARRIS / Builders Virtual CAD Conference, BIM Panel Discussion, Denver, Colorado, March 3, 2006.

22 Complete digital BIM models are currently provided by software such as Revit Architecture, CATIA, ARRIS, ArchiCAD, MicroStation, GenerativeComponents, and others.

23 BIM building awards, AIA Technology in Architectural Practice committee, or TAP.

24 Vladimir Bazjanac, "Virtual Building Environments (VBE), Applying Information Modeling to Buildings," Conference on Product and Process Modeling in the Building, 2004, 1.

25 BodyMedia, Extreme Textiles: Designing for High Performance exhibition, Cooper-Hewitt, National Design Museum, Spring 2005.

26 Chris Kasabach, interview, June 3, 2006.

27 Elaine S. Silver, "GSA to Require Building Information Models by FY 2006," Engineering News Record, January 21, 2005, http://enr.construction.com/news/informationTech/archives/050121.asp; Kristine Fallon (2007 Chair AIA TAP committee), interview, January 17, 2007.

28 Luciana Burdi, in a lecture in the GSD "CadCam2" course taught by professor Daniel Schodek, April 24, 2006.

29 Joann Gonchar, "Tech Briefs: To Architects, Building Information Modeling Is Still Primarily a Visualization Tool," Architectural Record, July 2006, http://archrecord.construction.com/features/digital/archives/0607dignews-2.asp.

30 AIA Technology in Architectural Practice (TAP), Prospectus 2006.

31 Douglas Paul, conversation regarding AIA TAP committee, January 16, 2007.

32 W. H. Mason, "Introduction to Airplane Design," Virginia Tech Aerospace and Ocean Engineering, 2001, 4. (Note: The average design time for a new airplane is five years.)

33 Paul Bezier, "Mathematical and Practical Possibilities of UNISURF," Computer Aided Geometric Design, 1974, 127–52.

34 Bruce Lindsey and Frank O. Gehry, Digital Gehry: Material Resistance, Digital Construction (Berlin: Birkhäuser, 2001).

35 The Solar Decathlon is a competition hosted by the U.S. Department of Energy in which twenty teams of college and university students compete to design, build, and operate the most attractive, effective, and energy-efficient solar-powered house, http://www.solardecathlon.org/about.html.

36 William Massie, chair of the Department of Architecture at Cranbrook; Berkeley-based Thom Faulders of BEIGE; the Canadian firm Forsythe + MacAllen Design Associates; Evan Douglis Studio in New York City; SHoP Architects in New York City; John Nastasi, director of Product-Architecture Lab at the Stevens Institute of Technology; and Byoung Soo Cho Architects of Seoul, Korea.

37 Nancy Solomon, "The Hopes and Fears of Design Build," Architectural Record, November 2005, 1.

38 Building Research Establishment Ltd., Scotland, "DTI Construction Industry Directorate Project Report: Current Practice and Potential Uses of Prefabrication," Department of Trade and Industry Report, No. 203032, 2003, 9, 14.

39 U.S. Census, 2005, http://www.census.gov/prod/2006pubs/07statab/pop.pdf; The Freedonia Group, "World Prefabricated Housing to 2004," 2001, http://www.freedoniagroup.com/pdf/1370smwe.pdf.

40 Jennifer Siegal, *Mobile: The Art of Portable Architecture* (New York: Princeton Architectural Press, 2002), 21.

41 Sears Archives, "What is a Sears Modern Home?," Sears, http://www.searsarchives.com/homes.

42 Andrew Blum, "Plug+Play Construction," Wired, January 2007, http://www.wired.com/wired/archive/15.01/home1.html.

43 Donald Olen Cowgill, "Mobile Homes: A Study of Trailer Life," *American Sociological Review* (August 1942): 573–74.

44 Bryan Burkhart, Phil Noyes, and Allison Arieff, *Trailer Travel: A Visual History of Mobile America* (Salt Lake City: Gibbs Smith Publisher, 2002), 39.

45 Richard Curtin, "The RV Consumer: A Demographic Profile 2005 Survey," Recreation Vehicle Industry Association, 2005, http://rvia.hbp.com/itemdisplay.cfm?pid=47 (accessed January 2007).

46 Christopher Deam, Design of Breckenridge Perfect Cottage, http://www.breckenridgeparkmodels.com/perfect_cottage.php, 2006; Christopher Deam, Design of Airstream, CCD International model, http://www.airstream.com/product_line/travel_trailers/intccd_home.html, 2004.

47 Stewart Taggart, "The 20-Ton Packet," Wired, October 1999, http://www.wired.com/wired/archive/7.10/ports.html.

48 B. Joseph Pine II, *Mass Customization: The New Frontier in Business Competition* (Cambridge, MA: Harvard Business School Press, 1992).

49 Daniel L. Schodek, Martin Bechthold, James Kimo Griggs, Kenneth Kao, and Marco Steinberg, *Digital Design and Manufacturing: CAD/CAM Technologies in Architecture* (New York: John Wiley & Sons, 2005).

50 U.S. Census, 2005, http://www.census.gov/prod/2006pubs/07statab/pop.pdf.

51 Ibid.; The American Moving and Storage Association, 2006, http://www.moving.org/before/smartmoving.html (accessed January 2007).

52 See Richard L. Florida, *The Rise of the Creative Class and How It's Transforming Work, Leisure, Community and Everyday Life* (New York: Basic Books, 2004).

53 Mark Weiser, "The Computer for the 21st Century," *Scientific American*, September 1991, 94–104.

54 Harry Stockman, "Communication by Means of Reflected Power," Proceedings of the IRE, October 1948. Cited by J. Landt, "Shrouds of Time, the History of RFID," Association for Automatic Identification and Data Capture Devices, 2001, 1196–1204, http://www.aimglobal.org/technologies/rfid/resources/shrouds_of_time.pdf.

55 Christian W. Thomsen, *Visionary Architecture: From Babylon to Virtual Reality* (New York: Prestel Publishers, 1994), 172–73.

56 Banwari Mittal, "I, Me, and Mine—How Products Become Consumer's Extended Selves," *Journal of Consumer Behavior 5*, no. 6 (2006): 550–62.

57 Anthony Alofsin, *The Struggle for Modernism: Architecture, Landscape Architecture, and City Planning at Harvard* (New York: W. W. Norton & Company, 2002).

58 Michael Sorkin, "Brand Aid, Or, the Lexus and the Guggenheim (Further Tales of the Notorious B.I.G.ness)," *Harvard Design Magazine*, Fall 2002/Winter 2003, 17.

59 Peggy Deamer, "Branding the Architectural Author," *Perspecta* 37: *Famous*, 37, (2006): 44.

60 Ibid.

61 OXO International, "Awards," http://www.oxo.com/oxo/about_awards.htm.

62 Michael Graves has designed more than eight hundred products for Target.

63 Randall Walter, architect, Bensonwood Homes, interview with the author, April 10, 2006.

64 John Habraken, keynote speech, Global Place: Practice, Politics, and the Polis conference, Taubman College of Architecture and Planning, University of Michigan, January 4, 2007.

65 Frei Otto, foreword, *Shigeru Ban*, Matilda McQuaid (New York: Phaidon Press, 2006).

66 Ali Rahim, *Catalytic Formations: Architecture and Digital Design* (New York: Taylor & Francis, 2006), 3.

PART TWO

PRACTICES:
ARCHITECTURAL
AND ENGINEERING
APPLICATIONS
OF DIGITAL
DESIGN AND
MANUFACTURING

CAD/CAM IN THE BUSINESS OF ARCHITECTURE, ENGINEERING, AND CONSTRUCTION

André Chaszar and James Glymph

This essay summarizes an interview with James Glymph of Gehry Partners focusing on the potential ramifications of computer-aided design (CAD) and computer-aided manufacturing (CAM) for professional practice including "organizational, contractual, and legal issues facing designers who wish to better integrate their work." Some of the questions addressed include the blurring of ownership and responsibility for digital information during the design and construction processes. The growing movement to establish a "master digital model" is discussed primarily in terms of the fabrication of complex building forms and components rather than as an information management tool—as is the case with building information modeling (BIM).

The advanced descriptive, analytical, and communicative capabilities of digital tools are encouraging their ever wider adoption in the building industry, which is now beginning to come to grips with the practicalities of leveraging the computing power that has revolutionized the industrial design, electronics, aircraft, boat-building, and auto industries. A significant number of architects have been encouraged by these technologies to propose and undertake projects of much greater complexity (whether formal, organizational, or both) than are found in conventional contemporary practice, and the engineers and builders with whom they work are correspondingly challenged to bring CAD/CAM to bear in their own work. But it is precisely this concept of "their own" work that poses the largest questions, the greatest challenges: in blurring the lines between architecture, engineering, and building, what becomes of the lines of ownership and responsibility?

Decades, even centuries, of effort have gone into creating the present sets of regulations and contractual forms governing the design and construction of buildings. Older still are the concepts of property that are an underlying motivation of much human activity. Digital working, on the other hand, implies (if it does not demand) a significant transgression of many of these boundaries. Certainly a good number of the most significant digitally produced buildings have, in one or more respects, succeeded by bridging over these barriers, allowing these projects to make the most of interdisciplinary collaboration and in many cases the elision of normally distinct building functions. Should all digitally produced works strive to do the same? What can architects, engineers, builders, building owners (perhaps even regulators and attorneys) do to facilitate such blurring where it is deemed desirable?

To be sure, questions like these are not entirely unique to the building industry. Ever widening adoption of the internet has raised a host of intellectual property issues, and a burgeoning branch of legal effort is emerging to address these. On the other hand, many of the other industries to which the digital evangelical in architecture point as exemplars do not face the same hurdles. Specifically, the aircraft and automotive industries, as well as industrial design producers (of consumer goods, and so on) tend to encompass the entire conception and production in-house, with only limited outsourcing. Design-build, if you will. Boat-builders differ somewhat, more nearly approaching the fragmented supply chain typical of building construction as noted earlier, and they are therefore perhaps a more relevant example to architecture, though their logistical challenges are still not as extensive. Yet the problems in building persist. The architects develop a digital model which their various engineering and other consultants can readily analyze and, where necessary, reconfigure. Assuming that after all of the modifications are made someone can check that the design "documents" (are they drawings, models, digital, physical?) are correct: Who owns the design? Say that constructability and other logistical and economic factors are successfully addressed through early involvement of the contractors: Who is responsible for "means and methods"?

Rethinking the procurement process required to fully exploit CAD/CAM's advantages leads generally to design-build as the preferred paradigm, in which many of the customary defensive obstacles are mitigated or eliminated by sharing financial risk and reward. Whereas the conventional "throw it over the fence" organizational model does at least have the advantage of giving fairly hard and fast rules about responsibility and the compensation for accepting it, the seamless flow envisioned by digital working methods requires much greater flexibility (and perhaps agility) from the participants. James Glymph says that the success of a collaboration among architects, engineers, and builders depends to a great extent simply on their willingness to "throw away the rule book" and streamline the flow of information and ideas where they see mutual advantage in doing so. Often, if the majority of the project team proposes to work this way, the building owner will go along with this.

As an alternative, Glymph reminds us that recent studies in the United States have indicated that negotiated-bid (or "construction manager [CM] at risk") contracts result in only slightly greater cost and time but much greater client satisfaction than does design-build. In order to effect this, architects can in some cases work from the outset of a project (or special part of a project) with contractors able to use CAD/CAM effectively, negotiating a price and allowing the design to evolve longer into the construction documentation phase. In so doing they may eliminate conventional documentation and its attendant production costs, duplication of effort, and inaccuracies in large measure.

Within a more conventional procurement scheme, architects can prequalify contractors with CAD/CAM capability, recognizing that they must also accommodate conventionally skilled ones for particular aspects of the project. Success on this front depends largely on the designers' abilities to either produce fabrication information that the contractors can use with confidence or find contractors who have already converted to digital production. Frequently the result is not a less expensive project but an equally expensive though more complex one, and the amount of the designers' time required for troubleshooting is substantial.

In any procurement scheme, then, architects and engineers can aim to design mainly in 3-D and derive the required 2-D documents (as needed by building officials, some non-CAM-capable contractors, and so on) from 3-D models, in order not to incur a large premium for duplicated effort. This of course requires software with appropriate capabilities "out of the box" or jury-rigged in-house. The former is less prevalent and the latter more so, leading all but the most committed designers to continue working in 2-D, but the emerging availability of better tools with more seamless modeling-drawing integration and object-oriented data structures means that we can look forward to more widespread adoption of "whole building" digital models in the coming years, with more promiscuous information-sharing as a result. [Fig. 1]

What sorts of checks and balances can the project team bring to bear in order to maintain the quality of their work in such fluid

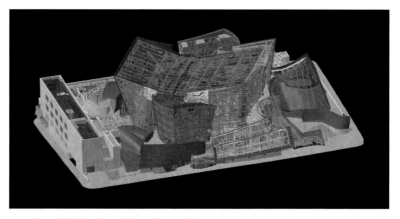

Fig. 1 / Digital 3-D modeling of the building's architectural, structural, and environmental systems shows an advanced state of coordination among design disciplines and building trades, which also enables negotiation of conflicting requirements. Walt Disney Concert Hall, Gehry Partners, Los Angeles, California, 2003, Courtesy of Gehry Partners, LLP circumstances? Some sort of "master model" in digital format is essential, says Glymph. Typically this model will describe the primary geometric characteristics of the project and, in the case of components that are "digitally contracted," also the scope of the work as a quantity output from the model. Sometimes the geometric relationships are definable by rules (as in parametric relational modeling) and in this case it may suffice to transmit these rules to each of the project's participants for them to reconstruct their own copies of the model. In the absence of such rules, as with "point clouds" and other highly complex spatial data, the individual data points themselves must be transmitted to all concerned. In either case it is then the responsibility of each party to verify the accuracy of the model upon which they will build their own components of the project.

Of course, updating the master model and all derivative models will be necessary as the project evolves, and the amount of effort and degree of reliability associated with these updates is a matter of significant concern. Clearly the updating process is easiest when all parties use a common modeling platform (and in some cases consultants' and contractors' participation in the project may be made contingent upon obtaining the requisite software), but this is not always possible. Parametric and similar modeling capability may also be preferable when design changes are definable as incremental rather than wholesale modifications. Let us bear in mind, though, that the entire issue of design change notifications is not well resolved in the building industry generally (visualize the difficulty of spotting individual but not always explicitly specified changes by overlaying physical drawings or layers of digital drawings), so we can expect that digital technologies will perhaps improve upon and not degrade current performance if proper contract standards are developed. In the short term, and for project teams not yet wise in the ways of digital production, it is possible that the rate of increase in complexity (of buildings or just of data structures) outpaces the improvement in the ability to coordinate complexity.

The significance of these advances depends on which participants (in the design, engineering, and fabrication process) develop the complete technical model. To get the most from this approach architecture and engineering teams need to be more aware of fabrication issues but, as pointed out by Glymph and others, many architects simply do not want the level of involvement (and corresponding control and responsibility) that the CAD/CAM continuum can offer. It is true that architects typically do not have, nor perhaps even want, the skills required to specify means and methods of construction. However, they can synthesize the abilities and coordinate the efforts of contractors, suggest construction systems and design within, or nearly within, the constraints imposed by available means of production supported by accurate (digital) documentation that contractors can rely on. Where successful, this method can result in improved economy as well as more ambitious designs, because much of the contractor's effort expended in interpreting and re-presenting the design becomes unnecessary.

For those architects and engineers who do take on this expanded area of responsibility, careful consideration is necessary of the skills required to produce reliable data for digitally driven manufacturing, lest they end up producing and "owning" a pile of scrap, as cautioned by Tim Eliassen in his article in the "Blurring the Lines" series in *Architectural Design* magazine.[1] Currently there are only limited technological means of assuring such quality. Instead, it is a matter of designers acquiring the necessary knowledge through formal or informal education, ranging from early exposure to such issues in their university coursework through opportunities to practice at the entire design/detail/fabricate continuum on the job, and perhaps even to internships or other practical experience in the employment of CAM-capable builders. (This is not a new prescription, by the way, but only a reiteration of a long-standing call for designers to reacquaint themselves with the problems of building in order to be more effective designers, a call now lent additional weight by the integrative potentials of CAD/CAM.)

The outcome of the emerging power of information technology, in Glymph's view, is that architects should leverage their improved design and communication capabilities in order to continue to be able to offer "architectural design"—that is, inclusion of attention to human factors—at an acceptably low premium. Otherwise building owners may resort exclusively to ordering buildings from design-build firms which will be able to design facilities using parametrized models of building types, for example. Thus, the ultimate questions are not about how to use computers but: Who will take best advantage of them, and what will be the effect on the built environment?

To summarize, existing contract forms require some modification, to encourage information flow among the parties involved in a project and best realize the advantages of CAD/CAM, if the current multiparty model of project-team composition is to survive, such as where architects work with contractors through a CM at risk. Education of designers requires some modification to better qualify them for working within such procurement processes. Collaboration between architects, engineers, fabricators and contractors must be encouraged, beginning in schools. Sadly, the opposite is often the case today—at both the educational and professional levels. Software (and to some extent hardware) must continue to develop in the direction of more useful functionality (both general and building-oriented), more transparent and reliable data-transfer among applications, and better user interfaces that do not require extensive programming skills in obtaining useful results with reasonable effort.

And as for the revolutionary impact of new materials and fabrication processes, it seems likely these will take care of themselves inasmuch as human inventiveness continues to unearth heretofore unimagined materials and processes and continues to rediscover and reapply old ones. [Figs.2–4]

André Chaszar is a Hungarian architect, an engineer licensed in New York, and an adjunct assistant professor of architecture at Columbia University who has published widely on the topic of digital design in architecture.

Jim Glymph is a partner with Gehry Partners and chief executive officer of Gehry Technologies, a company formed in 2002 to supply parametric design software solutions for the architecture, engineering, and construction industry.

Notes

1 Tim Eliassen, "Blurring the Lines" (series), *Architectural Design* 73, no. 3, (May/June 2003): 4.

Fig. 2 / Laser-cut model of Der Neue Zollhof apartments, Frank O. Gehry Architects, Düsseldorf, Germany, 1999, Courtesy of Gehry Partners, LLP

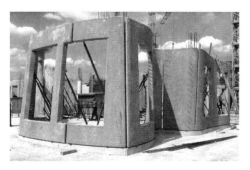

Fig. 3 / The shape of panels challenges conventional forming and reinforcing practices, requiring close collaboration between designers and contractors. Der Neue Zollhof apartments, Frank O. Gehry Architects, Düsseldorf, Germany, 1999, Courtesy of Gehry Partners, LLP

Fig. 4 / CNC milling of foam to create unique forms for concrete casting enables complex shapes while keeping costs acceptable. Recyclability of the foam also helps in cost control as well as addressing environmental concerns. Research is required by both designers and contractors to identify a suitable construction method. Der Neue Zollhof apartments, Frank O. Gehry Architects, Düsseldorf, Germany, 1999, Courtesy of Gehry Partners, LLP

COMPLEXITY AND CUSTOMIZATION: THE PORTER HOUSE CONDOMINIUM – SHOP ARCHITECTS

Amanda Reeser Lawrence

This short essay is a case study of SHoP Architects' groundbreaking project for the digital design and fabrication of a metal cladding system for their 2003 addition to an existing brick warehouse in Manhattan. Author Amanda Reeser Lawrence describes the firm's unique design approach and the strategy for this project in which SHoP "reconceptualized technology—both material and digital" in the design of the project's four thousand uniquely shaped panels.

With backgrounds spanning art to business administration, New York architects Sharples Holden Pasquarelli (SHoP) bring a unique set of skills to each of their projects. As a result, creative problem solving has become a kind of signature. Where Eero Saarinen once called for a "style for the job," SHoP instead offers a "solution for the job." In the case of the Porter House Condominium (2003), this attitude generated a design that incorporates innovative contemporary materials into a project with a limited budget by using and reconceptualizing technology—both material and digital.

Fig. 1 / The addition is cantilevered to the south of the existing structure, Porter House Condominium, SHoP Architects, New York, New York, 2003

The Porter House is an addition to an existing warehouse in the Meatpacking District of Manhattan, which adds fifteen thousand square feet and four stories to the original yellow-brick structure. [Fig. 1] Working with developer Jeffrey M. Brown Associates, SHoP bought the air rights from the adjacent building lots, enabling them to cantilever the addition eight feet to the south of the existing structure. While adding valuable square feet, this cantilever also helps define the new construction as an independent volume, rendered in a distinctive skin of zinc panels, floor-to-ceiling windows, and translucent light-boxes, which turn on automatically each evening.

This zinc panel system was custom-designed in collaboration with the engineering firm Buro Happold. Zinc was chosen for its high durability and rich material qualities, as well as its industrial aesthetic. A sharp contrast to the yellow brick of the original structure, zinc also appears on a new awning placed at street level.

After SHoP learned that outsourcing fabrication would be prohibitively expensive, they decided to manufacture the panels themselves. Beginning with a standard one meter by three meter sheet of zinc material, SHoP devised a system of three typical panel widths, such that the original zinc sheet could be cut into either one large sheet, two medium sheets, or three small sheets. From this seemingly simple

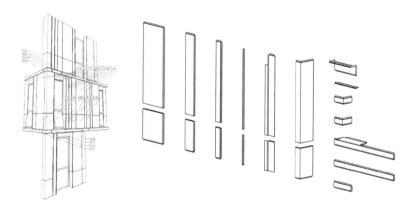

Fig. 2 / An axonometric detail of a building corner describes the different panel sizes as well as their installation sequence and location. Porter House Condominium, SHoP Architects, New York, New York, 2003

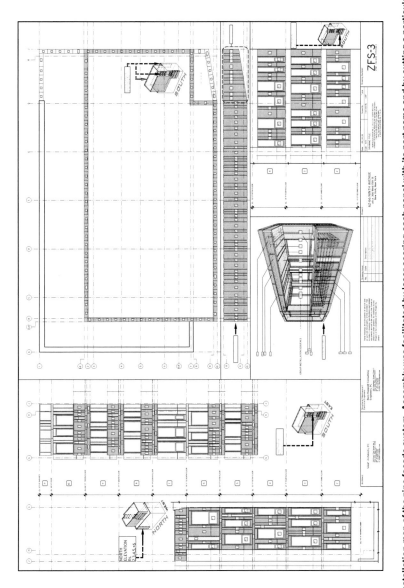

Fig. 3 / An installation map of the zinc facade system. Assembly was facilitated by laser scoring each panel with its part name and by cutting a particular hole layout in the panel to ensure that it was fastened in the correct location. Porter House Condominium, SHoP Architects, New York, New York, 2003

Fig. 4 / The installed panels, a process that required less than ten weeks
to complete, Porter House Condominium, SHoP Architects, New York,
New York, 2003

starting point, four thousand uniquely shaped panels were generated to accommodate various design specificities. Many of the panels were bent to perform three-dimensionally (as return profiles at windows, or as parapet caps, and so on) while others were designed to account for the varying floor heights and idiosyncrasies of the existing building. [Figs.2+3]

Perhaps the most significant aspect of the entire design and construction process was the absence of traditional shop drawings. Instead of transferring the design to dimensional drawings which describe each piece to be fabricated—an impossible task given the number and variation of parts—the design was instead transferred directly to the cutting machine through various software programs. SHoP first modeled the project in Rhino, then brought their design into SolidWorks, a program that can re-model a three-dimensional object when new dimensions are added into an Excel worksheet. Finally, a different software program was used to "nest" the dimensions onto panels, optimizing the amount of material used from each panel and allowing the firm to purchase nearly exact amounts of the relatively expensive zinc material.

As it was ultimately realized, the Porter House facade is composed of a matrix of zinc panels (three widths), floor-to-ceiling windows (four widths), and lightboxes (two widths); this design and construction was possible only through innovative use of digital and material technologies. [Fig.4]

Amanda Reeser Lawrence is an architect and an assistant professor of architecture at Northeastern University. She is also cofounder and coeditor of the architectural journal *PRAXIS*.

REMAKING IN A POSTPROCESSED CULTURE

William Massie

In this essay, William Massie describes the digital revolution that has led to a new and richer process of "remaking," which he defines as "quite simply the ability to move directly from information to work, marking for the first time man's ability to use abstraction as more than simply a container or vessel of intent." Referring to theorists and philosophers like Marshall McLuhan, Paul Virilio, and Gilles Deleuze, Massie connects architectural innovations with larger ideas concerning evolving relationships between the virtual and the real. Among his arguments is an assault on the concept of the "prototype" and its ties to mechanical standardization.

Viewed against the backdrop of epochal changes registered in industrial technology, architectural technology, since late modernism, seems to have ceased evolving. The development of new technologies, methods and materials, unrelated to existing ones, gives architects little recourse to historical techniques and representations. Despite the heterogeneity of current movements and theories, architectural discourse remains principally concerned with the ideology of all things retinal. Technology was long ago severed from the autonomy of architectural art. An abundance of practical and intellectual constructs have been erected around identical building techniques, producing in mainstream architectural culture an unbroken tectonic and representational tradition three decades old. Once again we see the institution of architecture dealing with arguably the most important spatial technology (the computer) in only a visual way. Some applications of computer technology have radically redefined how one sees and conceptualizes the making of space. Until recently, general use of the computer has been relegated to the world of the "virtual," as well as that of analysis. However, recent advances in electronics and computer processing found in computer numerically controlled technologies now allow us to move directly from a computer model/computer drawing to built form, This technology not only eliminates the distance between "virtual" architectural hypotheses and the physical test of construction, but also forces us to examine our roles as architects in a condition allowing greater potential input into the processing of building construction.

—WILLIAM MASSIE, 1997

If one suggests that the inception of modern process coincides with the Industrial Revolution, the trajectory of modern process to date can be cleaved into three distinct political dispositions: making/information transfer/remaking. This body of modern process defines not only our political and sociological predicament, but also what we have understood as modernism in terms of architecture.

The first iteration of modern process occurred with the advent of industrialization. Industrial culture to postindustrial culture can be described as the process of abstraction transmuted into object or space via mechanical means, with a bifurcation implicit in the process and the political power structure, that is management and maker. A technological and sociopolitical gulf existed between abstraction and making.

The second evolution of the development of modern process is the postindustrial information culture or the information-to-information culture which is defined by the transposition of abstraction to abstraction. This period of information transfer results in the commutation of ideas to ideas without transcending ones and zeros. Information is transposed from virtual to virtual. The flow and development of abstract ideas, through information systems and programming, provides the ability to redirect the mechanical to produce and maintain further abstraction. During this period corporations (dot-coms) were created simply to prove the capabilities of dispersing and retrieving information.

The third phase of this transformation is quite simply the ability to move directly from information to work, marking for the first time humanity's ability to use abstraction as more than simply a container or vessel of intent. Prior to the industrial era, architects were the purveyors of the built. As a result of the Industrial Revolution, industry itself became the purveyor of the built. In the progression toward the information culture, the practice of architecture was logically stripped from its base of technical expertise, transforming into an information-to-information politic—design to drawing. It is now individuals who are the purveyors of the built based on the power given to them by the infrastructure of remaking.

Remaking is based on the idea of multiple iterations of the process of "making." A construct is "made" digitally and then "remade" in the real—similar to the remixing of music. Drawing, space, or a body of text are constructed within a digital realm and then reissued into the physical world. These constructs can be altered within the digital and then preformed. According to Marshall McLuhan, "the consumer becomes producer in the automation circuit."[1] With the removal of traditional mitigating forces, the individual has direct access to information. If we use Home Depot as an example, the basis of the demystification of the construction industry is based not only on information transfer, but its result as a marketplace. Home Depot becomes the theater of operations for material comparison and experimentation because of its size and complexity of product. The individual moves through its aisles as though moving through a three-dimensional catalogue, attempting to synthesize difference in material options, unlike the traditional acquisition of material through specification. Paul Virilio in *A Landscape of Events* quotes Nicholas Negroponte of the Massachusetts Institute of Technology (MIT) and John Perry Barlow, president of the Electronic Frontier Foundation, as stating:

We have entered the digital age, the age of a universal network with
no one in charge, no president, no chief....Because of the network's
decentralized structure, it will be impossible to censor it without
banning the telephone! And this is a good thing, for cybernetic space
should reflect a society of individuals.[2]

Virilio goes on to state, "With the new means of transportation
and transmission, the new virtual tools, it is man who gives himself
wildly extravagant dimensions and the earth that reveals its limits."[3]

The information is the product, or to again quote McLuhan, "The
media is the message."[4] The information culture has evolved into a
"postprocessed" culture where information can directly result in the
product via information systems. The virtual moves directly into the
actual while the actual simultaneously reinforms the virtual. The relationship of initial abstraction has been processed to anticipate the real.
Prior to this point information was processed only to produce a further
abstraction—information systems, that is the internet. "Postprocessed"
information exists simultaneously as a product because it can move
directly into the "real." Information is temporally suspended within
the virtual (latent information) until it is realized physically. Pushed
from the world of physics, into the paradigm of making, "potential
information" is transposed into "kinetic information." The very anticipation of the real is, in a sense, like a back eddy in a stream—although
the energy of the water is moving predominantly in one direction, the
pressure on an object within the stream produces a reverse flow—a
perforation in the virtual that allows the actual to penetrate and move
back into the system, folding in on itself or imploding, a type of endless loop unaware of its container, either virtual or actual, simply a
blending of the two. The result of this blending of virtual and actual
is not only embedded in itself, but causes the blending of virtual to
virtual conditions—new transformations of existing power structures,
technologies, and information systems. A traditional understanding of
"job site" and the anticipation of "construction" can be drawn back
into digital space where an object is not only drawn but is embedded
with a series of activities, politics, and sequences. The infrastructure
and intelligence of the office presents itself to the site. The scripting
of assembly and the corporal choreography fold back into what could

have been considered drawing. When an author produces a drawing that becomes the information that drives the machine, it compresses the world of design and fabrication into a single process, thereby yielding efficiencies not realized in the industrial era. This concept is reinforced by McLuhan in *Understanding Media*, in which he describes the discourse that takes place between the two realms (virtual and actual) as a complex nervous system capable of receiving data from the outside and transmitting it for reprocessing—an "organic unity of interprocess."[5] McLuhan goes on to state that the "instant synchronization of numerous operations has ended the old mechanical pattern of setting up operations in lineal sequence...mechanical standardization is now past."[6]

With the end of standardization and the transfer of power to the individual achieved through the ability to move directly from information to construct, the idea of the prototype—the first in a series—becomes obsolete. Architect Bernard Cache has discussed this effect in *Earth Moves*, in the sense that an object, which exists within the virtual, is "malleable in real time" and has thus "lowered the status of the prototype" due to the ability to produce a series of continuously changing complex forms.[7] The new information systems and processes utilizing non-Euclidean geometries allow infinite variation and the development of a nonstandard mode of production. According to Cache, since design occurs as a 3-D simulation and this simulation can be milled, the simulation takes precedence over the physical object. It should be argued that in fact the virtual simulation and the physical object are one and the same with no hierarchy. Since the virtual exists simultaneously as the real, the concept of infinite variation replaces the model of the "prototype." The prototype is simply replaced by type—the death of "proto"—and the concept of standardization is no longer viable. As Gilles Deleuze writes in *The Fold*:

> The new status of the object no longer refers its condition to a spatial mold—in other words, to a relation of form-matter—but to a temporal modulation that implies as much the beginning of a continuous variation of matter as a continuous development of form....The object here is manneristic, not essentializing: it becomes an event.[8]

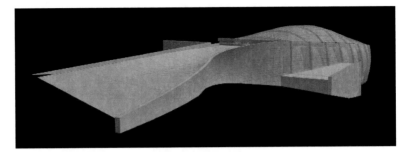

Fig. 1 / Through a global positioning survey, the foreground and background topographies were drawn together to produce the parent geometry of the Big Belt House, Willam Massie, White Sulfur Spring, Montana, 2000–2002

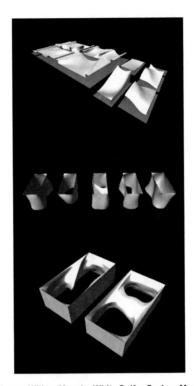

Fig. 2 / Big Belt House, Willam Massie, White Sulfur Spring, Montana, 2000–2002. Top: The transformation of mass as it relates to the reformation of light has no prototypical condition. It simply "is" and "projects." Middle: The hardening of light, that is the projection, aperture/container is tested, retested, and combined with other tests prior to its actual construction. Bottom: The dissection of the light container is the last step of the digital process and the first step in material negotiation.

Fig. 3 / Detail view of aggregate PVC tube construction, steel sections of
the actual construction are transposed from the original form as select nodes
in a spline geometry. Big Belt House, Willam Massie, White Sulfur Spring,
Montana, 2000–2002

Fig. 4 / Aggregate PVC tube construction combined with overall stress-skin panel construction, Big Belt House, Willam Massie, White Sulfur Spring, Montana, 2000–2002

The practice of architecture is and will remain primarily an information system, but architecture within this given phase of modern process is transforming as a result of the radical shift in the conception, production, and communication of ideas and subsystems. The transformation into an electronic culture is as socially and politically significant as the development of written language. The advent of what McLuhan refers to as an alphanumeric system altered the political and social structure due to its ability to disseminate information and to create decentralized power structures. The utilization of digital information systems, the concept of information working through the use of numerically controlled processes—bits to atoms—allows the individual to move directly from abstraction to object without typical meditation.

Historically, to develop a system of a certain complexity, that is a spatial construct which is not easily described by Euclidean geometry or the juxtaposition of the rectilinear and the measured, required an unwieldy amount of information to be transmitted from designer to fabricator, making such projects economically prohibitive. Through the use of the computer and computer-numerically-controlled technologies, this complex information moves directly from idea to product. Due to these technologies the individual obtains increased control relative to the production of ideas. The ability for direct dialogue between virtual and actual provides a substantial increase in artistic autonomy. With the removal of traditionally mitigating forces in the logistics of architectural production, the onus of accountability received by the architect becomes greater. [Figs. 1–4]

William Massie is currently the architect-in-residence and head of the architecture department at Cranbrook Academy of Art in Bloomfield Hills, Michigan. He is also a tenured architecture professor at Rensselaer Polytechnic Institute.

Notes

Epigraph William E. Massie, "The implications of corporal occupation of a virtual construct: a work in progress," *Architecture and New Geographies of Power*, ACSA Western Regional Meeting, Washington State University School of Architecture Publications and Printing (Pullman, WA), 1997, 37.

1 Marshall McLuhan, *Understanding Media: The Extensions of Man* (Cambridge, MA: MIT Press, 1999), 349.

2 Paul Virilio, *A Landscape of Events* (Cambridge, MA: MIT Press, 2000), 8.

3 Ibid., 10.

4 McLuhan, *Understanding Media*, 7.

5 Ibid., 348.

6 Ibid., 349.

7 Bernard Cache quoted in Alicia Imperiale, *New Flatness: Surface Tension in Digital Architecture*, (Basel, Switzerland: Birkhauser, 2000), 59.

8 Quoted in ibid., 90.

ENGINEERING OF FREEFORM ARCHITECTURE

Harald Kloft

This essay catalogs a collaborating engineers' reflections on the vari-ety of digital design and construction challenges posed by innovative architects and complex designs. Case studies of projects by Bernhard Franken, Frank O. Gehry, and Peter Cook are discussed in terms of each architect's unique design process and the engineering and fab-rication issues that arise during the process of collaboration. Areas of focus include the challenges of geometry creation, data transfer, and structural analysis. Of particular interest is the topic of structural optimization and each architect's relative degree of willingness to alter or manipulate their formal proposals in response to structural performance issues. These range from Gehry's insistence on sculp-tural envelopes within which the load-bearing structure is hidden to Peter Cook's willingness to allow structural behavior to contribute to shaping his buildings during the design development process. In an extended postscript, Kloft analyzes subsequent trends in the develop-ment of freeform buildings.

Departures from basic geometries in architecture have historically often coincided with the development of new materials. This correlation is obvious in the 1950s, '60s, and '70s, during which developments in concrete and later plastics inspired architects and engineers to treat form in a less restrained manner. The lack of suitable design and manufacturing tools, however, frequently confined designers to regular geometries. Recent years have seen a renaissance of free forms—designers today are formally less constrained as a result of modern computer technology. This essay explores structural design issues in the context of three geometrically complex projects based on experiences I made as leading project engineer in the office of Bollinger + Grohmann in Frankfurt, Germany:

> The Dynaform, the BMW pavilion for the 2001 International Auto Show in Frankfurt by architects ABB/Bernhard Franken
> The MARTa (museum of contemporary art and design) Herford (2005), Germany, by Gehry Partners
> The Kunsthaus Graz (2003), Austria, by architects Peter Cook and Colin Fournier

The translation of a freeform into a built structure requires the development of new modes of thinking from all project participants. It is essential that architects and engineers collaborate from the very beginning of a project. In the case of freeform architecture an important aspect of this collaboration is that the structural engineer has to "speak the language" of the architect and fully support the particular design approach. Understanding individual design values in my opinion means that discussions with architects such as Bernhard Franken, Frank O. Gehry, or Peter Cook will be of a very different nature.

Form Finding Process

The form finding processes of these three architects vary distinctly. Bernhard Franken and his team rely heavily on computational tools to generate the shape. [Fig. 1] In the beginning of the project Franken has no preconceived formal idea. His "parametric design process" starts with a briefing by the client about the communication concept for the exhibition. Franken translates program- and site-specific parameters

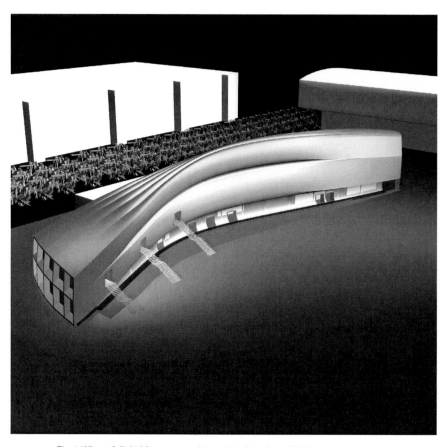

Fig. 1 / View of digital form generation model, Dynaform BMW pavilion, ABB
Architekten/Bernhard Franken, 2001

into virtual forces using software environments such as Maya. In case of the 2001 International Auto Show in Frankfurt, BMW's primary interest was the presentation of the new BMW 7 Series. Franken set up a three-dimensional matrix that was initially shaped according to the virtual forces of a driving car, hence the influence of the program. Adjacent buildings on the site such as Nicholas Grimshaw's Frankfurt Trade Fair Hall (2001) further impacted the shape through a series of specially designed force fields. The initial shape was deformed and altered by the Maya software, until the design parameters in Franken's opinion were sufficiently represented. The approximate shape was corrected for geometrical errors and established the 3-D master geometry of the project. This master geometry provides the dimensional reference for all project participants during design development and construction. Franken refers to the BMW pavilion as a freeform figure called Dynaform.

Frank O. Gehry's MARTa Herford, in Herford, Germany, illustrates a different approach. Here the design process does not start out in a virtual design environment; instead, the architects manually build a series of physical models, many of which are 3-D-digitized in

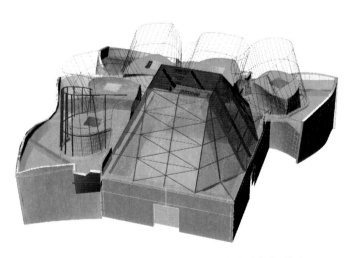

Fig. 2 / Digital model of structural design, MARTa Herford, Gehry Partners, Herford, Germany, 2005

Fig. 3 / Digital structural model and aerial view, Kunsthaus Graz, Peter Cook and Colin Fournier, Graz, Austria, 2003

order to correct and check the shape with respect to program and site in a computer-aided design (CAD) environment. The CAD-corrected data enables the building of more accurate physical models that often explore the implementation of the overall shaping strategy in partial and more detailed models of the project. [Fig. 2] Gehry generally concentrates on the effects of the exterior surface and the interior spaces, and relies largely on physical models to verify that the original design intent is met. The most important difference from Franken's form finding process is that Gehry does not define a 3-D master geometry as a dimensional reference before starting the design and structural development. Rather form finding turns out to be a kind of "iteration process" in which form changes are digitized and refined.

Peter Cook's and Colin Fournier's design for the Kunsthaus Graz, in Graz, Austria, illustrates the third approach. Here, the conceptual design phase during the architectural competition does not rely heavily on computers, and physical models that represent the complex roof shape are handmade. The 3-D digital model generated during design development is shaped to capture the design intent of the original scheme. [Fig. 3] While following the initially proposed shape, it is built independently and does not contain digitized data taken directly from the physical models like Gehry does.

Structural Design

What are the implications of these different design approaches for structural design? In all cases it is important to bear in mind that our analytical software tools and the 3-D design environments that architects use do not normally share a common digital structure or database. Thus it is in the interest of the engineers to develop "post-processors" that automate and accelerate the file transfer mechanisms. Inputting geometry manually is impractical and time-consuming for complexly shaped structures. Being able to import files accurately and quickly enables engineers to directly apply finite-element and spatial-vector programs to problems that need to be solved during the design process.

In Franken's approach we are given the external surface as the master geometry of the project. We generally have two options for developing the structure: we either design a system of linear or curvi-linear structural members that support a secondary and nonstructural skin, or the skin itself is conceived as the primary load-bearing system and becomes "skin deep"—a surface-structure with shell-like behavior. Since the master geometry is fixed, we cannot optimize the structure through modifications of the overall shape. High local forces or bending moments have to be accepted: a structural optimization of the overall shape would call the underlying design approach into question. Rather the aim is to bring forces in a "dynamic balance" to support the idea that form is "only a frozen moment."

In Gehry's project we are given the database of the outer and inner surface and the interstitial space "between" results to integrate a structural system and embed all necessary mechanical elements. The load-bearing structure—often a series of steel frames—is hidden from the user and architecturally almost irrelevant. In this "undercover role" the main part of structural engineering is a geometrical optimization that means to identify the layout of structural members in the interstitial space and optimize the arrangement so that it works in a structural way. The internal and external surfaces themselves act as enclosures without any primary load-bearing function; their geometry establishes boundary parameters for us that cannot generally be changed.

Peter Cook, unlike Gehry and Franken, creates the digital model when translating his scheme from the conceptual status to a design development phase in a digital environment. Though the objective is to remain close to the original shape, Cook does not pursue this process dogmatically. And in contrast to Franken's forms the structural behavior could have influence on the shape, driven by the idea of possible structural systems and the understanding of their behavior. In the case of the complex roof for the Kunsthaus Graz the principle task was to design a system of tubular steel members that support an outer layer of complexly shaped acrylic glass sheets. This external skin is designed as a series of discrete layers, each responding to a specific set of functional requirements. The structural layer, in response to the need for creation of a stiff and minimal structural system, arranges members in a triangulated pattern.

Manufacturing

Lack of suitable materials and production techniques are problems that anyone seeking to design and build freeform surfaces will, at some point, be faced with. Building regulations and standards that do not cover new procedures and materials, and potentially high construction costs add to the difficulty of constructing a complex shape. Since buildings are normally one-of-a-kind structures, we cannot apply industrial processes that may be well suited for the production of complexly shaped parts but require large quantities in order to be economical. Presenting the manufacturing processes for some of Bernhard Franken's BMW pavilions illustrates my experiences with issues in the manufacture of freeform structures.

The BMW pavilion for the 1999 International Auto Show in Frankfurt, the Bubble, follows the form of two merging liquid drops consisting of waterjet-cut aluminum that support a transparent Plexiglas skin. [Fig.4] Three hundred different spherical Plexiglas sheets were thermoformed over computer-numeric-control-milled polyurethane foam molds at temperatures of 150° to 160° Celsius. The edges of each sheet were trimmed to the designed shape after the forming process. Each foam mold was milled several times for the forming of individual sheets. Full-size testing of the manufacturing process and a full-size mock-up of the assembly are essential for a new manufacturing process, such as the one described, to be successful. [Fig.5] We initially wanted to glue the sheets together without any primary frames, but had to abandon the idea after full-size testing only six weeks before the scheduled opening of the pavilion revealed unforeseen difficulties. The aluminum frames now actually make the

Fig. 4 / Exterior view of the Bubble BMW pavilion, ABB Architekten/Bernhard Franken, 1999

Fig. 5 / Slump forming acrylic panels on CNC-milled molds for the Bubble BMW pavilion, ABB Architekten/Bernhard Franken, 1999

shape of the pavilion visible and are generally considered as a design feature that enhances rather than disturbs the shape of the pavilion.

In 2000 Franken and his team designed a second BMW pavilion, this time an interior structure for the auto show in Geneva. A double-layered network of aluminum pipes is supported by an enclosing set of steel pipes—all curved in two directions. The flexible aluminum tubes were manufactured with a single curvature and were bent on-site into their doubly curved shape, a procedure tested beforehand with a full-size assembly mock-up. The tubular steel members are significantly stiffer and could not be formed in the same way. Instead, each steel pipe was subdivided into up to one hundred single-curved segments that were aligned, rotated, and welded together into the desired over-all geometry. Accurately bending a tube to a defined radius is actually very difficult—and much time was spent in designing the details such that tolerances in the bending radii could be compensated for in the connections between segments.

The last example is the manufacturing of the 2001 BMW project—the Dynaform described above. After much discussion and the evaluation of different options, we decided to separate the primary load-bearing structure from the structurally secondary skin and design a series of primary steel frames. Franken's team generated fifteen cross-sections through the master geometry, each at a different angle and each resulting in a unique shape. We then inscribed structural frames—so-called Dynaframes—into these sections. [Fig.6] The outer line of the Dynaframes precisely follows an offset of the master geometry surface, while the inner line represents the reversal of the same master shape. At regular intervals both lines are connected with welded plates for working in a structural way as a vierendeel system. These plates all point to the origin of form generation—the virtual curvilinear path generated by a car driving through the space. The design of the rather strange seeming Dynaframes thus originates in the general form finding principles of the scheme and is not primarily driven by a structural logic.

The steel members for the frames were cut from flat steel plates, then bent into shape and manually welded together. [Fig.7] The contractor was faced with the challenge of having to maintain tight tolerances while translating our accurate 3-D data into a built shape. A

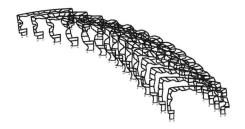

Fig. 6 / Digital view of structural bents, Dynaform BMW pavilion, ABB Architekten/
Bernhard Franken, 2001

Fig. 7 / Fabrication of structural bents, Dynaform BMW pavilion, ABB Architekten/
Bernhard Franken, 2001

full-size mock-up of several structural frames was completed in May;
it enabled us to study the required assembly time and procedures as
well as identify and resolve problems with the connections between
certain components.

The exterior of the pavilion is meant to be the purest possible representation of the master geometry. A major concern was to find a way
of constructing a skin that would generate a smooth surface over the
complex shape. After researching different material options we finally
decided to use a pre-tensioned polyvinyl chloride (PVC) membrane.
A specialist for structural membranes, Viktor Wilhelm from Stuttgart,
developed a method for generating a ruled surface with single curvature from the given geometry of the cross-sectional frames. By modeling the skin as a ruled surface we avoided any external folds, and the
membrane could be prestressed between the structural frames. After
the design team and the client approved the envelope concept on a
full-size mock-up in Pilsen, Czech Republic, specialists with moun-
tain climbing training began with the erection of the membrane. Each
span between adjacent steel frames was covered with one membrane
segment. The joints between membranes were sealed with an apron
fabric—a compromise as far as the overall appearance is concerned,
but unavoidable with respect to the tight construction schedule and the
need for a watertight envelope.

An architecturally difficult question was how to design and
produce openings in a large smooth and complex shape such as the
Dynaform. Here the solution was to intersect the surface with a second surface shaped according to the desired opening, and allow this
surface to project beyond the external skin of the surface of the master
geometry. The opening becomes an independent formal element and
begins to resemble an airplane wing or a gangway.

The finished project looked effortless, with materials and
shapes seeming to connect almost naturally. Designing and building
a large freeform structure such as the Dynaform requires more
energy, time, and creativity than would be necessary for a normative
structure. Deadlines, the budget, and the design intentions cannot
be compromised. The BMW pavilion remained in place for the duration of the auto show, was then disassembled, and is now stored for
future use.

Postscript

Concerning the content of my essay from today's perspective, I would like to classify my experiences of engineering freeform architectures more precisely in three more or less distinct categories regarding the role of structural design: shaping form, finding form, and generating form.

Shaping form in my definition means a design process with an analogous use of digital tools. There is no interaction between the planning the parties desired in regard to changes of the formal design. The design process is more or less defined as a linear increase in detailing of the architectural idea. Logically, designing a structure in such a planning process begins after the architectural design and is not intended formally to change the shape. From that point of view architectural design is not related to the structural logic of form, but structural design is nevertheless a key factor in realizing the architectural idea. Shaping form can be described as a "top-down process" to articulate the formal architectural idea and design the most efficient composition of geometry, structural system, and materiality. Examples of this mode of collaboration in structural design are the described projects with Bernhard Franken (Bubble and Dynaform) and Frank O. Gehry (MARTa Herford).

In contrast to the described process of shaping form where structural optimization is not allowed to instigate formal changes, *finding form* is an interactive process of using digital tools. In the processes of finding form architectural design is open for careful geometrical changes of the initial shape. However, both shaping form and finding form share the common basis that the starting point of structural design is positioned after formulating the architectural idea and therefore implementing structural logic is more or less efficient. One example that illustrates this process of finding form is the collaboration with Peter Cook and Colin Fournier on the design of the Kunsthaus Graz. In contrast to the idea of shaping form, Cook and Fournier supported structural optimization by careful alterations of the shape with respect to their architecture. Therefore, the structural behavior was allowed to have an influence on the final geometry.

Another example of this category of finding form is the Kloepp (2003, unbuilt), a project of Franken\Architekten and the Office for

Structural Design (o-s-d) for a new building to house three ministries in Reykjavík, the capital of Iceland. In this project the architects did not define strictly a master geometry as in the Bubble or Dynaform projects; quite the opposite: the geometry, especially in the facades, was subject to change as the project developed. The architectural design was done digitally as in Franken's earlier projects, using Maya. The conceptual origin, as inscribed into the parameters of the initial digital design process, was found in the fissured surfaces of Iceland's topography and in a stone monument near the site, inside which, in accordance with the Icelandic legends, elves live. The process of form finding was highly iterative with interactive use of tools: the initial form, architecturally generated by sampling time-based processes modeled in Maya, was structurally analyzed using finite-elements software. After interpreting the results, the form was optimized geometrically while adhering to the initial design intentions in a joint process with the architects. Our engineers at o-s-d took on Franken's design approach as a special challenge and combined the idea of the programmatic distortion of the facade with the actual flow of forces. The architects agreed to develop the facade as the primary support structure, which bears both the vertical loads and acts as a reinforcing element to provide high earthquake resistance. What lends the building its strong impact is that the final design of the shape and facade are in harmony with the actual flow of forces. After finishing the detail planning, the client stopped the project, but the building is still in discussion to be realized.

The third category, *generating form*, aims for an integrative design process where structural design issues are part of the architectural concept. This process aims for a collaboration between architects and engineers from the very beginning by an integrative use of digital tools. The challenge of generating form is to combine architectural and engineering creativity right from the beginning of a project and integrate structural design parameters in a "bottom-up process." The design for a roof construction for a bus station in Wädenswil, Switzerland, exemplifies the process of generating form and marks a new step toward integrative design processing. [Fig.8] At the beginning, the Berlin-based architectural team of Kuhn + Steinbächer Architekten designed a roof structure based on a formal idea responding to technical and site-specific requirements. At the same time, the shape was implemented in the engineers finite-element software to examine the structural behavior with the aim to optimize the shape in regard to the geometrical stiffness (so-called shell-like behavior). After this first run a second process of optimization started in regard to the efficiency of the structural system itself. The aim was to design a highly efficient use of materials by not varying the heights or width of the structural elements but by generating an inner porous structural system. By using modern computer numerically controlled (CNC) production technologies a "structural porosity" was generated by cutting holes in the flat steel elements where the pattern exactly followed the calculated stress flow. The designed structural system visualizes a logic of form, whose lightweight character is obviously sensible and behaves quite free compared to the traditional requirements for an economic structural system.

The described collaborations on freeform architectures represent new opportunities in building. Besides the formal freedom that new computer technologies offer, digital design tools also hold the promise of new collaborative design synergies for architects and engineers. In this context, structural engineers may redefine the creative potential of their discipline. An important aspect of the emerging collaborative design synergies is that structural engineers have to speak "the language of the architects" and architects have to show an interest in structural principles. Understanding individual design values is essential for a promising integration of engineering potential in architectural design.

Finally, reading my manuscript six years after its first publication, besides content two things spontaneously come to my mind: First, I had incredible luck to be at the right time in the right place to have had the fantastic chance to engineer those freeform architectures. The experiences I made in the beginning of the twenty-first century were very diverse and I am still profiting from the knowledge I got in that period of my life. Second, the Dynaform project symbolizes a temporary peak in realized, digitally designed architectures for BMW as well as for Bernhard Franken and me. Although, the construction of the Dynaform was designed for reuse in the succeeding auto shows, after 2001 BMW changed the priorities in exhibition design and in 2003

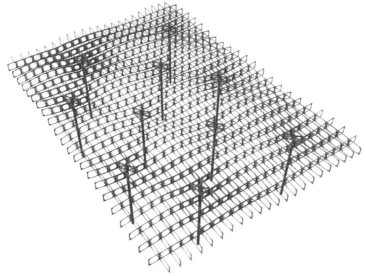

Fig. 8 / Form follows efficiency: generated "structural porosity," bus station, Kuhn + Steinbächer Architekten, Wädenswil, Switzerland, 2008

built a new fair pavilion, an unspectacular "box," which was rebuilt in 2005 and 2007. What happened? It is noticeable that in research is a continuous development in digital design tools, such as the introduction of parametric modeling systems to automate design processes or the propagation of plug-ins for scripting in different software tools. Additionally, the implementation of CNC-manufacturing processes in building increases continuously. But this development is not the same as a progression in realized freeform architectures, and projects like the Bubble and the Kunsthaus Graz still mark the peak in using sheet plastic.

What could be reasons for this development? Peter Eisenman, in a lecture titled "On the Problem of Late Style," referred to the evolution of architecture with its continuity of sign and meaning besides the developments of architectural style and presented the conclusion that we are in a period of "lateness," when things get tired and are without any meaning.[1] Some of his statements are quite remarkable: "We are teaching performance but no competence to produce meaning. Parametric design today offers infinite options, but contemporary architectures show no variations.... In all moments of lateness, there is always the possibility of the new, but an avant-garde is needed to symbolize a paradigm shift and to create a new architecture."

In my opinion, the introduction of "new architectures with meaning" is always connected to new developments in technology. In the past, paradigm shifts in architecture were always synchronous with developments of new materials. But defining a new architectural style loaded with sign and meaning is a process that occurs over decades or longer, too. Looking back in history at the beginning when a new material was found, designers had no examples and ideals for its use in building and therefore had no formal language for the material. For example, the famous Iron Bridge at Coalbrookdale (1779), England, which passes as the first cast-iron bridge, had the shape of a classical stone bridge, even if constructed without stones, and the detailing of the joints followed the principles of wood constructions. But with its lightness the bridge expressed the new. And the development in materials from cast-iron to steel structures brought a continuous formal shift in architecture over the last two hundred years. Or concrete: Nervi's formal expression of the potential of concrete structures is based on a continuous development of concrete technology and architectural design.

Actually, the development in digital tools emerges as the catalyst of an upcoming paradigm shift in architecture. Today, it is possible to produce all effects and visions in the digital world but the challenge is to bring the digital world into reality and especially to become architecture. Whereas in earlier times the qualities of materials guided designers to create architecture, in digital design infinite options of form could be produced without any connection to material properties. And, developments in materials were always connected to sociological, economical, political, and cultural developments and defined the so-called logic of form. In contemporary architecture we don't have reasons for logic of form, and form without reasons has no meaning and is, according to Eisenman, no architecture. In my opinion, actually we don't need new materials to introduce meaning in contemporary architecture. We "only" have to connect digital and real worlds by materializing the digital. Only by introducing material properties and manufacturing issues in the digital process of form generation in so-called bottom-up processes will we be able to introduce meaning in today's architecture. To materialize the digital world creates the chance for new arrangements and compositions of materials, so-called nonstandard constructions, which has the potential to lead to a more differentiated and appealing, as well as a more resource-efficient, building culture. In a computer-driven planning and production environment, variety and irregularity no longer go against the idea of efficiency. Rather, local variations in structures become possible, which in turn allow for other types of efficiency. By responding more closely to actual local needs, more complex structures may increase resource efficiency at the same time.

Broadly speaking one could describe this shift as one from the industrial age to the information age. Architectural design in the information age aims to integrate as much information as possible at the beginning of the planning process by creating "Bottom-up 3-D models" as active instruments in an integral design process. These digital models are informed from the beginning with all relevant issues, so that architectural design is tuned to technical feasibilities as well as to sociological, economical, cultural, and environmental requirements.

Additionally, bottom-up 3-D models should be designed as complex information structures, which allow designers to optimize their design models iteratively throughout the entire design process. All together, we are on the digital way from performance to competence but this needs time.

Harald Kloft is an engineer and principal of the Office for Structural Design (o-s-d) in Frankfurt, Germany. He is also chair of the Department of Structural Design in the Faculty of Architecture at the University of Kaiserslautern, Germany.

Notes

1 Peter Eisenman, "On the Problem of Late Style," lecture, Graz, Austria, September 24, 2008.

MASS CUSTOMIZATION AND THE MANUFACTURE MODULE

James Woudhuysen with Stephen Kieran and
James Timberlake

This essay is an interview in the form of a conversation between Stephen Kieran and James Timberlake—authors of the widely influential book Refabricating Architecture: How Manufacturing Methodologies are Poised to Transform Building Construction—*and James Woudhuysen, coauthor of* Why Is Construction So Backward? *Although the focus is clearly on* Refabricating Architecture, *the overall discussion addresses the wider debate surrounding the business implications of new technologies in the design and construction industries.*

Reading *Refabricating Architecture* is a joy. When so much divides America from Europe, or at least appears to divide the two, here are the principals of KieranTimberlake, in Philadelphia, upholding transatlantic unity. They explain how, in 2013, a notional Boeing Worldwide Constructs factory, based on the firm's 38-hectare (95-acre), eleven-story room in Everett, Washington, could airlift massive subassemblies of buildings to global destinations—with the help of Airbus jets.

Ah, those subassemblies. "The more one attempts to undertake at the point of assembly," the authors note, "the more difficult it is to control quality."[1] *Refabricating Architecture* is a confident, vivid, and irrefutable case for moving construction into the world of supply-chain management, upgradeable services, and buildings as quilts, with hardly any joints to be made on-site.

The book is also a paean to information technology (IT). Historically, architecture has relied on flat drawings to convey a construction—plans, sections, elevations, and details. These 2-D representations of 3-D buildings would be better simulated: "Simulation makes possible the fragmentation of large artifacts, such as aircraft, into large, integrated components that can be fabricated anywhere in the world and brought together for final assembly."[2]

I wondered what practical experiences had made Stephen Kieran and James Timberlake write the book, and how it had been received in the United States.

"From the beginning," says Timberlake, "our practice has been based in craft, and in construction, and the careful integration of the two. Over the past decade we'd become disappointed with the level of quality of the craft, as executed: not only our own, but within architecture at large."

In response to this, at the University of Pennsylvania, where they run a final-semester master of architecture design research laboratory, the partnership began exploring ways to increase architectural quality through the integration of disciplines around new materials and methods. In late 2000, they wrote a proposal to the College of Fellows of the American Institute of Architects. The college was sponsoring, for the first time ever, a research fellowship—the Benjamin Latrobe Research Fellowship. Kieran and Timberlake won that first fellowship, and decided then to write up their research in a document that eventually became *Refabricating Architecture*. From the start, the intention was to write theory based on the current, factual state of architecture and construction. The authors wanted to instigate change, and in that spirit *Refabricating Architecture* has been enthusiastically received within academic circles.

But what about their theory as it applies to their everyday practice? "We are now beginning to see the architecture profession and the construction industry pick it up," continued Timberlake, justifiably proud.

> It has resonated among some in the development community, where
> monetary carrying costs can be the difference between doing a project and shelving it. And like *Why is Construction So Backward?*, we
> wanted to prompt changes within the profession. Both of our books
> begin at the same place, but take quite different patterns to the end.
> We both seek better craft, quality, and design. We are in agreement
> that under the present design, supply, construction and procurement
> arrangements, without change, architecture and construction face a
> regressive future and more disappointment rather than success.[3]

Architecture needs to think bigger when it comes to modules, and develop the logistical means for handling them. Kieran and Timberlake have realized that although cars, planes, and ships move through space, buildings, which will always remain relatively static artifacts even after delivery and installation as manufactured modules, are often smaller. They ask: Why can't buildings go through the kind of giant-scale modular assembly processes that exist at Kvaerner's Philadelphia shipyard?

As a practice, KieranTimberlake is obviously influenced by the successes and ambitious scope of U.S. transport design. So why had they omitted to consider techniques for manufacturing railway trains?

In fact, they love trains, and wish Amtrak had selected a manufacturer from Europe with a proven design rather than specifying and procuring a design inferior to that of rolling stock in Europe. The focus of *Refabricating Architecture* on automobile, aircraft, and shipping manufacturers was partly, according to Timberlake, to do with "ease of access to the plants, to people and processes. Also, the three reinforce our argument about scalability—sheer size and numbers. And they exhibit nice differences in supply-chain characteristics, modalities, and assembly methods."

In any case, there are only so many arguments you can handle at once. "Folks criticize our book for instancing the automobile industry, because they believe it represents mass production rather than mass customization. [Fig.1] In reply, we hold up the wonderful example of

Fig. 1 / Diagram of the relationships between quality, scope, cost, and time, modified from the original in *Refabricating Architecture* to include environmental responsibility, © KieranTimberlake

Bentley cars. They are truly bespoke—we love that word—and so clearly represent mass customization. Train manufacturing has the scale, and some of the processes, but we weren't sure that it truly represented the best examples of the theory we were trying to explain."

I said I thought Bentley cars were an example of customization without the preface "mass," but we soon moved on.

One of the great things Kieran and Timberlake do is ridicule those who say that manufacturing methodologies are a pipe dream as far as construction is concerned. I like the way they attack previous attempts in the genre as "automating mediocrity." But, allowing for poetic license, how do they reply to skeptics who don't believe that U.S. industry will make the advances suggested by 2013? As the pair hint, U.S. off-site fabrication, in giving the world the concept of "trailer trash," has done neither itself nor the domain of housing any favors.

"U.S. construction has a long way to go, and 2013, seven years from now, might be optimistic," confided Timberlake. "Unlike the manufacturing models we chose, construction is highly fragmented, from the supply chain through to procurement. Of course, too, the design profession is separated from the construction industry—unlike the manufacturers with integrated design capabilities we focused upon. Last, the U.S. government is disinclined to involve itself in private companies or industry, so there is little impetus for change from the government, unlike, for instance, the United Kindom or Japan. The U.S. modular housing industry is clearly behind many Japanese and European manufacturers in terms of CAD/CAM, integration and production."

Kieran and Timberlake are optimistic, however. They are keen on several bright stars in the construction industry:

- Skanska, which has experience in Europe with offsite technologies[4]
- Capsys, a company building multifamily prototypes in a Brooklyn, New York, shipyard[5]
- Kullman Buildings, New Jersey, which builds ambassadorial outposts for the U.S. State Department off-site, and ships them around the world[6]

• Jacobs Engineering Group, in Charleston, South Carolina, which, with high-quality off-site techniques, fabricates upmarket clean laboratories—also for shipment worldwide[7]

Each of these examples is helping to change how the United States and international construction industries will act, think, and produce. But Kieran and Timberlake are a little too quick to abandon mass production as "the ideal of the early twentieth century." They assert that mass customization "is the recently emerged reality of the twenty-first century," and argue that this is cultural production rather than the making of industrial outputs.[8] By cultural production they mean that, rather than decide among options produced by industry, the customer "determines what the options will be by participating in the flow of the design process from the very start."[9]

I agree with them that the advances of Dell are fantastic, although no other computer manufacturers have been able to emulate its ability to tailor PCs to what buyers ask for. Kieran and Timberlake also know the book *Digital Design and Manufacturing*. That book seems to be more accurate when it prefers the term "personalization" to "customization." With personalization, buyers are able to choose configurations only from options that have been predetermined by manufacturers.[10]

In response, Timberlake again cites Bentley, adding to this the BMW z4.[11] He insists that "the first is true mass customization; the second is an example of design integration, with possibilities for late changes in the production stream. Both occur within industries that are upheld as paragons of mass production, not customization."

Warming to this theme, he continued: "Our communication software, our CAD abilities, and the supply-chain opportunities all exist to enable true mass customization to occur, which we think *Digital Design and Manufacturing* ignores. And isn't personalization really another way of saying mass customization?

"The existing construction industry already applies mass customization techniques to integrated component assemblies—bathrooms, kitchens, curtain walls, mechanical/electrical system components. These assemblies allow architects to customize or personalize the component for integration into a larger architectural composition. The

Permasteelisa Group, a global curtain-wall manufacturer based in the Veneto, Italy, deploys components from worldwide manufacturers, custom assembled to the specifications of the architects whose designs it executes.[12] It integrates engineering, design, and manufacturing to ensure high-end final products that look unique to each project, but in fact use many standard smaller bits within the kit supplied."

Myself, I remain more convinced that personalization is how the mass market tends to operate. I don't find anything especially cultural about architects abdicating responsibility for design decisions to customers. This plea for customer- and user-led design is all too familiar from the world of IT, and fails to convince. Although the phrase "master builder" is too loaded, Kieran and Timberlake are much nearer the mark when observing that "today, through the agency of information management tools, the architect can once again become the master builder by integrating the skills and intelligences at the core of architecture."[13]

To be fair, Timberlake was adamant that the duo don't want to abdicate design responsibility. Rather, "the opportunities for making adjustments, and program revisions, and final improvements, which in the past have notoriously stopped the design and production show, can now be an integral part of the process.

"We do advocate the return of authority and responsibility for design and control to the architect, as it once was, in the role of 'master controller.' We don't think we will be master builders again, at least in the sense of [Filipo] Brunelleschi five hundred years ago. But by embracing integration, collective intelligence, and the technological tools available to us, architects can regain the kind of control of processes they have not enjoyed for nearly a century."

There are other nuances in *Refabricating Architecture* that I wanted Kieran and Timberlake to justify: for example, their view that the making of architecture is "organized chaos."[14] Sometimes it seems that they nod approvingly, but in my view rather eclectically, to the doctrines of chaos and complexity. There is no need to try to dignify a rational case for modular subassemblies with these somewhat overblown ideas, wrenched from unrelated scientific domains.[15]

"Well, chaos and complexity are in our recent past, in that Robert Venturi and Denise Scott Brown were mentors of each of us during our early careers. Ours is less nodding approval than acknowledgement of the messy vitality the process of making architecture is...and in comparison to the more rational processes of the three nonconstruction industries explored by *Refabricating Architecture*, architecture and construction are indeed chaotic and complex!"

For Timberlake, there are three reasons for the anarchy that obtains.

First, architecture and construction remain processes with few overlaps—design and building only rarely overlap, because of the needs of the client, time constraints, and cost constraints.

Second, the fragmentation of design input adds to confusion. A multiplicity of consultants gets involved in the most basic of projects. Supplier inputs into construction, and different methods of procurement, make things worse. The result is that architecture is a nonlinear affair.

Last, Timberlake argues that, in *Why Is Construction So Backward?*, Ian Abley and myself had alluded to a similar chaos and complexity, and a lack of conformity to early craft. He notes our point that, to uphold a true return to craft, construction needs to embrace new technologies and methods for making.[16] But what we meant was not craft in the sense of the present use of construction trades, so much as a turn to manufacturing architecture—whether built like ships, simulated, modularized, and assembled like the Airbus A380, or assembled like production-run cars.

My final quibble was about Kieran and Timberlake's fondness for new materials. I, too, am a fan—but Ian Abley makes the point that there is plenty to be done with old materials as much as new ones.

Timberlake accepts this. More positively, though, he adds: "If today's new materials enable integration, lighter assemblies, and new technologies, then the world of design and construction will be enhanced by embracing them, rather than ignoring their possibilities.

"There used to be a saying around the American automobile industry: 'They don't make them like they used to.' That was a subtle hint that older was better. In the past decade, however, with the advent of new materials, systems, assemblies, designs, and technologies, automobiles have become better than ever."

Kieran and Timberlake want to take architecture to a completely new level by embracing new materials, systems, assemblies, designs, and technologies—an ambition they share with Ian Abley and myself.

James Woudhuysen is professor of forecasting and innovation at De Montfort University, Leicester, United Kingdom.

Stephen Kieran and **James Timberlake** are partners in the award-winning firm KieranTimberlake, and are both adjunct professors at the University of Pennsylvania School of Design.

Notes

1 Stephen Kieran and James Timberlake, *Refabricating Architecture: How Manufacturing Methodologies Are Poised to Transform Building Construction* (New York: McGraw-Hill, 2004), 87.

2 Ibid., 59.

3 James Woudhuysen and Ian Abley, *Why is Construction So Backward?* (Chichester: Wiley-Academy, 2004), 163.

4 Skanska, http://www.skanska.com (accessed August 10, 2005).

5 Capsys, http://www.capsyscorp.com (accessed August 10, 2005).

6 Kullman Buildings, http://www.kullman.com (accessed August 10, 2005).

7 Jacobs Engineering Group, http://www.jacobs.com (accessed August 10, 2005).

8 Kieran and Timberlake, *Refabricating Architecture*, xii.

9 Ibid., 111.

10 Daniel Schodek, Martin Bechthold, Kimo Griggs, Kenneth Martin Kao, and Marco Steinberg, *Digital Design and Manufacturing: CAD/CAM Applications in Architecture and Design* (Hoboken, NJ: Wiley, 2004), 156.

11 Bentley Motors, http://www.bentleymotors.com (accessed August 10, 2005); BMW Automobiles, http://www.bmw.com (accessed August 10, 2005).

12 Permasteelisa Group, http://www.permasteelisa.com (accessed August 10, 2005).

13 Kieran and Timberlake, *Refabricating Architecture*, xii.

14 Ibid., 53.

15 See John Gillott and Manjit Kumar, *Science and the Retreat from Reason* (London: Merlin Press, 1995).

16 Woudhuysen and Abley, *Why is Construction So Backward?*, 258–60.

PART THREE

REACTIONS AND PROJECTIONS: CRITICAL EVALUATIONS OF DIGITALLY MANUFACTURED ARCHITECTURE

SELF-ORGANIZATION AND MATERIAL CONSTRUCTIONS

Michael Weinstock

This essay focuses on "biological models" as inspiration for new material and structural approaches in design. The author describes the characteristics of self-organization, and gives special emphasis to the geometry of soap foams as a model for cellular arrangements at various scales—from bone tissue to building frames. He discusses material advances like foamed approaches to making lightweight but strong polymers, metals, and ceramics that are slowly finding applications in the construction industry. Structural analysis tools like form-finding are presented in terms of their debt to biological processes such as the self-organization of natural systems into stable arrangements under applied loading. Among his examples is the "water-cube" design for the 2008 Beijing Olympic swimming venue by PTW Architects with Arup. This project is described in detail concerning the use of the Weaire-Phelan approach to soap bubble mathematics in conjunction with computational scripting to develop and analyze structural form and performance.

In recent years, new strategies for design and new techniques for making materials and large constructions have emerged, based on biological models of the processes by which natural material forms are produced. Biological organisms have evolved multiple variations of form that should not be thought of as separate from their structure and materials. Such a distinction is artificial, in view of the complex hierarchies within natural structures and the emergent properties of assemblies. Form, structure, and material act upon each other, and this behavior of all three cannot be predicted by analysis of any one of them separately.

The self-organization of biological material systems is a process that occurs over time, a dynamic that produces the capacity for changes to the order and structure of a system, and for those changes to modify the behavior of that system.[1] The characteristics of self-organization include a 3-D spatial structure, redundancy and differentiation, hierarchy and modularity.[2] Studies of biological systemic development suggest that the critical factor is the spontaneous emergence of several distinct organizational scales and the interrelations between lower or local levels of organization, the molecular and cellular level, and higher or global levels of the structure or organism as a whole. The evolution and development of biological self-organization of systems proceeds from small, simple components that are assembled together to form larger structures that have emergent properties and behavior, which, in turn, self-assemble into more complex structures.[3] The geometry of soap foams is a model for the cellular arrangements at all scales in natural physical systems.

Natural Constructions

Natural materials develop under load, and the intricate interior structure of biological materials is an evolutionary response. At the level of the individual, there is also an adaptive response as, for example, bone tissue gets denser in response to repeated loads in athletic activities such as weightlifting. Bone is a cellular solid, a porous material that has the appearance of mineralized foam, and its interior is a network of very small and intricately connected structures.[4] When bone becomes less dense, due to age or prolonged inactivity, it is the very small connective material that vanishes, so that the spaces or cells within the bone become larger. The loss of strength in the material is disproportionate, demonstrating the importance of the microstructure: larger cells make a weaker material.

Cellular materials are common at many scales in the natural world, for example in the structure of tiny sea creatures, in wood, and in bones. What they have in common is an internal structure of "cells," voids or spaces filled with air or fluids, each of which has edges and faces of liquid or solid material. The cells are polyhedral, and pack all the available arranged space in a 3-D pattern. Foam has cells that are

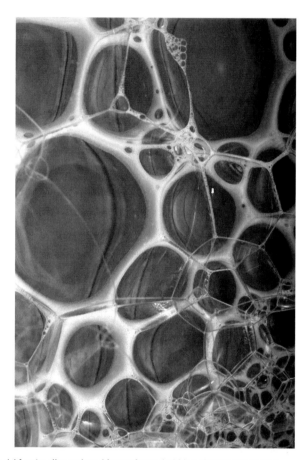

Fig. 1 / A naturally produced foam of soap bubbles, demonstrating the differentiation of polyhedral cells in an intricate geometry of foam architecture, including the basic plateau rules for the intersection of three films

differentially organized in space, whereas honeycombs are organized in parallel rows and tend to have more regular, prismlike cells. In all cellular materials, the cells may be either regular or irregular shapes, and may vary in distribution. [Fig. 1]

D'Arcy Thompson discussed the mathematical expressions for the shapes of growing cells in 1917, arguing that new biological structures arise because of the mathematical and physical properties of living matter.[5] His chapter "The Forms of Cells," when read in conjunction with the "Theory of Transformations," has been extended today to patterning and differentiation in plant morphogenesis. The problem of mathematical descriptions of foam has a long history, but it can be observed that foam will comprise a randomized array of hexagon and pentagon structures.[6] Diatoms and radiolara are among the smallest of sea creatures, and the intricate structures of their skeletons have fascinated, among others, Frei Otto and his biologist collaborator J. G. Helmke. It has been argued that the formation of these tiny intricate structures is a process of mineralized deposits on the intersection surfaces of aggregations of pneus or bubbles.

The Construction of Materials

In the industrial world, polymer cellular foams are widely used for insulation and packaging, but the high structural efficiency of cellular materials in other, stiffer materials has only recently begun to be explored.[7] Comparatively few engineers and architects are familiar with the engineering design of cellular materials, and this has contributed to the slow development of cellular structures in architecture.

Industrial and economic techniques do exist for producing foams in metals, ceramics, and glass. Foamed cellular materials take advantage of the unique combination of properties offered by cellular solids, analogous properties to those of biological materials, but they do not share their origin. They are structured and manufactured in ways that are derived from biological materials, but are made from inorganic matter. The production processes for metal foams and cellular ceramics have been developed for the simultaneous optimization of stiffness and permeability, strength, and low overall weight. This is the logic of biomimesis, abstracting principles from the way in which biological processes develop a natural material system, applying analogous methods in an industrial context, and using stronger materials to man-ufacture a material that has no natural analogue.

The ability of some materials to self-organize into a stable arrange-ment under stress has been the founding principle of structural form-finding in the physical experiments of Antoni Gaudí, Heinz Eisler, and Frei Otto. *Organization* here refers to the reordering of the material, or the components of the material system, in order to produce structural stability.

Biomimetics is essentially interdisciplinary, a series of collabora-tions and exchanges between mathematicians, physicists, engineers, botanists, doctors, and zoologists. The rigid boundaries between the inherited taxonomy of "pure" disciplines make little sense in this new territory. Similarly, the traditional architectural and engineering ways of thinking about materials as something independent of form and structure are obsolete.

New research into the molecular assembly of structures and mate-rials in what were previously thought to be homogenous natural mate-rials has led to biomimetic manufacturing techniques for producing synthetic materials, and new composite materials are being "grown" that have increasingly complex internal structures based on biological models. The fabrication of composites relies on controlling structure internal to the material itself, at molecular levels. Here, process-ing is the controlling parameter and growth is more than a metaphor. "Grown" materials are layered, molecule by molecule, to create dis-tinctive microstructures in thin films, making new combinations of metal and ceramic that are produced by design rather than "nature." New composites such as flaw-tolerant ceramics and directionally solidified metals might seem to be a long way from the materials avail-able to architects, but they are already in use in many other fields.

Other "designed" materials, such as polymers and foamed met-als, are already being used in many aerospace, maritime, and medical applications. Polymers also have unique combinations of properties not found in "natural" materials, being lightweight, very flexible, and mechanically strong. In tandem with their electrical and optical prop-erties, this makes them highly suited to military applications. In air-craft fuselages and body armor they offer high strength for low weight, providing structural stability and flexibility.

Simple polymers, such as the ubiquitous plastics like DuPont's Corian, are homogenous materials, similar in density and strength in all directions. Complex polymers need not be homogenous, and can be produced with surfaces that have different properties from the polymer interior. Complex polymers are useful for films and surfaces with multiple layers, each with distinct and differentiated functions. Manufactured by mimicking and adapting the self-organizing behavior and complex functions of natural polymers, very strong transparent or translucent films can be produced with a water-repellent and self-cleaning surface for facade systems. The process, known as "free living radical polymerization," can produce honeycomb structures at a molecular level, although the controlled formation of the honeycomb morphology at larger scales is still in the research, rather than production, phase.

Kevlar is perhaps the best-known manufactured organic fiber and, because of its unique combination of material properties, it is now widely used in many industrial applications. It has high tensile strength (five times that of steel), low weight, and excellent dimensional stability, and so has been adopted for lightweight cables and ropes in many marine and naval applications. Kevlar has high-impact resistance, so it is the major fiber constituent in composite panels in military and civil aircraft, and in sporting equipment such as canoes, skis, racquets, and helmets. However, it has yet to be used widely in architectural construction.

Liquid crystals have the flow properties of a conventional liquid, and the molecular structure of a solid crystal. This is a phase change occurring between the crystalline and isotropic liquid states. Kevlar is produced, in part, by manipulating the liquid crystalline state in polymers. Spiders use the low viscosity in the liquid crystalline regime for the spinning of their silk. Spider silk is as strong as Kevlar, which means that it has superior mechanical properties to most synthetic fibers and can stretch up to 40 percent under load. This gives it an unusual advantage, in that the amount of strain required to cause failure actually increases as deformation increases, an energy absorbing ability that allows the web to absorb the impact of flying prey.

Self-organizing materials, such as liquid crystals, natural polymers, and copolymers found their first applications in biotechnology, sensor development, and smart medical surfaces, and more recently in maritime, automotive, and aerospace applications, but they have the potential to produce new structures and systems for advanced architectural engineering.

There is new interest within the material sciences and industry in the use of ceramics as a structural material. Ceramics are very light, but their compressive strength matches, or exceeds, that of metals. They are hard and durable, resistant to abrasion, and noncorroding as they are chemically inert. Ceramics are good insulators (both electric and thermal) and can resist high temperatures. However, they have one major disadvantage: their lack of tensile strength. The solution to this problem is being sought in biological models—the forming of complex structures internal to the material—and as new production facilities come online ceramics may become the most ubiquitous of new materials for built structures. Cellular ceramics are porous and can now be manufactured in various morphologies and topologies, ranging from honeycombs and foams to structures woven from fibers, rods, and hollow spheres. Substitutes for human bone and the coating of orthopedic prostheses are produced by similar methods.

Injecting a stream of gas bubbles into liquid metals is the basic technique for producing foamed metals, but preventing the bubbles from collapsing is difficult. Adding a small quantity of insoluble particles to slow the flow of the liquid metal stabilizes the bubbles in the production of aluminum foam sheets, produced with open or closed cells on the surface. Aluminum foams can be cast in complex 3-D forms, are stronger and more rigid than polymer foams, can tolerate relatively high temperatures, and are recyclable and stable over time. They are very light, nominally about 10 percent of the density of the metal, and are currently used as a structural reinforcement material, particularly in aerospace applications, though they have not yet reached their full potential in lightweight architectural structures.

Closed-cell aluminum honeycomb is widely used as the core material of panel structures, conventionally with other materials as a surface. This is no longer strictly necessary, as new advanced processes produce "self-finished" surfaces of high quality. Cellular metals including, but not exclusively, aluminum, are being deployed for applications such as acoustic absorption, vibration damping, and innovative thermal regulation. As the frequency and range of applications increases, data accumulates for the relationship between the topology of cells in the foam and the subsequent performance of the cellular material, so that improved and optimized cell topologies can be produced.

Another new open-cell foamed material, made of a glasslike carbon combining properties of glass and industrial carbons, can be used for biological "scaffolding." Reticulated vitreous carbon has a large surface area combined with a very high percentage of void spaces, is sufficiently rigid to be self-supporting, and is biologically and chemically inert. Cellular glass structures are used in medical applications for bone regeneration. The bioactive glass acts as a scaffold to guide the growth and differentiation of new cells, and this requires an open-cell structure that is highly interconnected at the nanometer scale. The cells must be large enough to allow the bone tissue to grow between the cells, yet fine enough so that the "bioglass" material can be absorbed into the bone as it is replaced by living tissue.

Material Constructions

Design and construction strategies based on space-filling polyhedra and foam geometries offer open structural systems that are robust and ductile. Control of the cell size, the distribution and differentiation of sizes within the global structure, and the degree and number of connections are variables that can be explored to produce strength and permeability. SMO Architektur and Arup designed the Bubble Highrise (2002, unbuilt) by packing a notional structural volume with bubbles of various sizes, then used the intersection of the bubbles and the exterior planes of the notional volume to generate a structure that gives entirely column-free interior spaces. The Watercube National Aquatics Center (2006), Beijing, was designed by PTW Architects and Arup using a structural design developed from Weaire and Phelan's soap bubbles arrays. [Fig.2] Despite the appearance of randomness, the elements of the structure are highly rational and so economically buildable. [Fig.3] The Watercube is an enormous building, 177 meters (581 feet) on each side and more than 30 meters (98 feet) high. The network of steel tubular members is clad with translucent ethylene

Fig. 2 / Overall scale 177 meters (581 feet) by 177 meters (581 feet) by 30 meters (98 feet) high, with an entirely column-free interior space, digital rendering of the Watercube National Aquatics Center, PTW Architects, CSCEC+Design, and Arup, Beijing, 2006

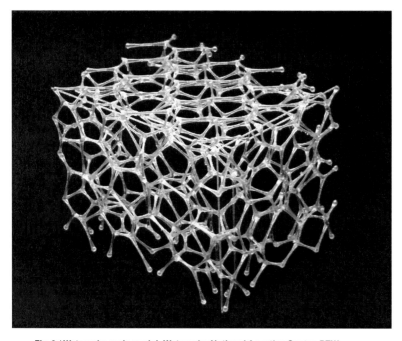

Fig. 3 / Watercube resin model, Watercube National Aquatics Center, PTW Architects, CSCEC+Design, and Arup, Beijing, 2006

Fig. 4 / Watercube cladding installation, Watercube National Aquatics Center, PTW Architects, CSCEC+Design, and Arup, Beijing, 2006

tetrafluoroethylene (ETFE) pillows. [Fig. 4] Over such a wide span of column-free space, the need to minimize the self-weight of the structure is paramount, as most of the structural work involves ensuring the roof can hold itself up.

The steel tubes are welded to round steel nodes that vary according to the loads placed upon them. There is a substantial variation in size, with a total of around twenty-two thousand steel members and twelve thousand nodes.

There is a total of four thousand "bubbles" in the Watercube, the roof being made of only seven variant types (of bubbles) and the walls of only sixteen variations, which are repeated throughout. The geometry was developed by extensive scripting, using the Weaire and Phelan mathematics, with a further script required for a final analytical and geometrical correct 3-D model. Scripts that run in minutes can deal with the tens of thousands of nodes and beam elements, and scripting was also used to develop structural analysis models and models from which drawings were automatically generated.

The ETFE cushions make the building very energy efficient, and sufficient solar energy is trapped within to heat the pools and the interior area, with daylight maximized throughout the interior spaces.

Conclusion

A systematic change is on the horizon, whereby the boundary between the "natural" and the "manufactured" will no longer exist. The complex interaction between form, material, and structure of natural material systems has informed new biomimetic industrial processes, generating new high-performance materials. New processes are having a compelling impact on many industries, and new materials are radically transforming aerospace and maritime design and medicine. Cellular materials, especially metals and ceramics, offer an entirely new set of performance and material values, and have the potential to reinform and revitalize the material strategies of architectural engineering and construction.

At the scale of very large architectural projects, the emphasis on process becomes not only the significant design strategy, but also the only economic means of reducing design data for manufacturing. Biomimetic strategies that integrate form, material and structure into a single process are being adopted from the nanoscale right up to the design and construction of very large buildings.

Michael Weinstock is an architect who, since 2006, has served as academic head of the Architectural Association School of Architecture in London, where he is also director of the Emergent Technologies and Design master's program.

Notes

1 Stuart A. Kauffman, *The Origins of Order: Self-Organization and Selection in Evolution* (Oxford: Oxford University Press, 1993).

2 "A combination of emergence and self-organization is often present in complex dynamical systems. In such systems, the complexity is huge, which makes it infeasible to impose a structure a priori: the system needs to self-organize. Also, the huge number of individual entities imposes a need for emergence." Tom De Wolf and Tom Holvoet, "Emergence and Self-organization: A Statement of Similarities and Differences," *Proceedings of the 1st European Conference on System Science*, 1989.

3 Francis Heylghen, "Self-organization, Emergence, and the Architecture of Complexity," *Proceedings of the 1st European Conference on System Science*, 1989.

4 The structure and properties of cellular solids such as engineering honeycombs, foams, wood, cancellous bone, and cork have similarities of behavior and can be exploited for engineering design. Case studies show how the models for foam behavior can be used in the selection of the optimum foam for a particular engineering application. See L. J. Gibson and M. F. Ashby, *Cellular Solids: Structure and Properties* (Cambridge: Cambridge University Press, 1997).

5 D'Arcy Thompson, *On Growth and Form* (Cambridge: Cambridge University Press, 1961), first published 1917.

6 Joseph Plateau's observation in 1873 that when soap films come together, they do so as three surfaces meeting at 120°, and Lord Kelvin's 1883 challenge of subdividing a 3-D space into multiple compartments or cells. D. Weaire and R. Phelan, "A Counterexample to Kelvin's Conjecture on Minimal Surfaces," *Philosophical Magazine Letters* 69 (1994): 107–110. See also D. Weaire, "Froths, Foams, and Heady Geometry," *New Scientist*, May 21, 1994, 34–37.

7 Denis Weaire and Stefan Hutzler, *The Physics of Foams* (Oxford: Oxford University Press, 2001).

AUTOMATION TAKES COMMAND: THE NONSTANDARD, UNAUTOMATIC HISTORY OF STANDARDIZATION AND AUTOMATION IN ARCHITECTURE

Kiel Moe

This essay provides a cogent summary of the sociocultural factors underpinning the development of numerically controlled manufacturing processes as a basis for challenging readers to consider whether new developments in this area truly represent the kind of revolution that many proponents claim. By looking closely at the long history of technical developments in fabrication technologies, Kiel Moe challenges the notion that today's new technologies are unprecedented in their newness, and links them more closely with their roots in governmental, military, and corporate systems of control.

The aim of this essay is to present the assemblage of social, economic, cultural, and disciplinary factors that condition the use of digital fabrication in building design by briefly surveying the history of digital fabrication and its implications for architecture. It focuses on the concept of numerical control (o) and tracks how the concept evolved inside and outside of architecture from its archaic origins to contemporary design and fabrication methods. It is grounded in an assumption that techniques and technologies are socially and culturally determined and only become technical means thereafter. As Gilles Deleuze states, any technology is social before it is technical.[1] [Fig.1]

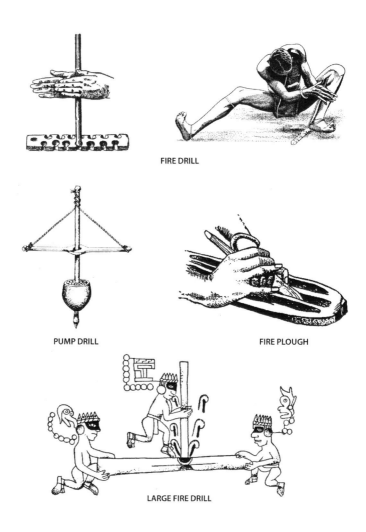

FIRE DRILL

PUMP DRILL

FIRE PLOUGH

LARGE FIRE DRILL

Fig. 1 / Modern digital fabrication techniques are automated versions of techniques that have ancient origins.

Numerical Control

The primary tools and techniques of digital fabrication appliances are familiar if not archaic. Take, for instance, the two most common cutting mechanisms in computer-aided design (CAD) and computer-aided manufacturing (CAM) technologies: the rapidly rotating router bit and the laser. The router bit is merely a refined application of the partial rotary motion tools, such as the fire drill, bow drill, and pump drill used as boring and cutting tools throughout the archaic world.[2] The laser involves the application of concentrated energy to sever molecular bonds, thereby cutting materials. This is an advanced form of the fire drill and fire plough: both cut with similar albeit less concentrated applications of heat energy.[3] These archaic technologies have undergone substantial refinement, especially through the mechanical and electronic paradigms of the nineteenth and twentieth centuries. However, their operative principles remain intact.

What is "new" in digital fabrication, and thus the source of much promise and interest, is the control of a tool along a path no longer guided by the neurological-muscular feedback loop of a human technician. Instead, it is now controlled by a path in a numerically defined blanket of points. Our current use of the term numerical control in digital fabrication was coined by the U.S. Air Force after World War II in their search for an elaborate manufacturing system capable of producing primarily repetitive and occasionally complex components for warplanes and weapons systems.[4] Numerical control is the technique that enables the CAD/CAM operations of digital fabrication processes, parametric design software, and the management of design information, as in the case of building information modeling (BIM).

This history of military enterprise in the 1950s and '60s is central to the digital fabrications techniques of current design practices but reflect only a few applications of a more general concept of numerical control. Numerical control is, first, a much broader concept that extends well-beyond nascent digital fabrication practices in architecture. The history of numerical control is a history of a technique that fundamentally is used to abstract properties into numbers in order to effectively regularize, routinize, and quantify that which is otherwise irregular, aleatory, and qualitative. There is no better term than *numerical control* to characterize the impetus of Western technics (that is, the history of our technical practices), capitalism, and our current paradigm of floating currencies, future markets, the proliferation of digital technologies of all types, or our current social paradigm, which German sociologist Ulrich Beck calls the "Risk Society."[5]

Thus, it is important to first establish the cultural preparation of numerical control practices in architecture and our adjacent disciplines. The following brief account of numerical control will establish where, when, and how the concept and implementation of numerical control developed. Numerical control is not new, but rather is a deep and pervasive characteristic of all that we call modern.

Mechanical Numerical Control Techniques

Although there were many notable numerically controlled economic and social devices throughout antiquity that helped regularize the aleatory aspects of life (calendars and calculators, for example), it was in the monasteries of the West that numerical control most powerfully emerged as a consistent technique of regularization and routinization.[6] With the clock and bell, the Benedictine monasteries at the beginning of the last millennium synchronized liturgical rites with the bell tower. This regularized the spatial and temporal behavior of the monks—but in doing so, also fundamentally transformed their experience of duration. Our physiological systems—no longer synchronized to the rhythms of the sun, seasons, and free morphogenesis—became increasingly determined by numbers. The numeric basis of technique would soon fundamentally alter many aspects of Western life by initiating an endless succession of quantitative methods used to coordinate human production of all sorts.

Numerical control techniques migrated from the Benedictine monastery clock-and-bell assembly into the clock towers of market centers in European towns to help organize commerce. As the emerging capital model of trade physically shaped Europe in the following decades and centuries, the incorporation of double entry bookkeeping was the next application of numerical control. Soon, devices and practices as diverse as cartographic techniques and the mathematics of planetary motion would do for space what the clock did for the regularization and standardization of time.[7] In architecture, Leon Battista Alberti's discovery and subsequent derivation of the laws of perspective, Claude

Perrault's quantification of the classical orders, Jean-Nicolas-Louis Durand's utilitarian utopia of grids, and Le Corbusier's regulating Modulor scale are each notable applications of numerical control that prepare digital fabrication techniques in architecture.

More broadly, several new techniques in the early Enlightenment further developed numerical control and accelerated the role of numeracy in design. The Flemish mathematician Simon Stevin made significant contributions by the use of decimals as well as what we now know as statics. At the beginning of the seventeenth century the Scottish scholar John Napier developed logarithms, a system for the numerical control of numbers themselves.[8] Slide rules accelerated calculation and the authority of the engineer's calculations soon followed into the design and fabrication fields.

As the burgeoning instrumentality of numerical control expanded in the West and proceeded into the industrial revolution, the famous Jacquard loom with its punched card programs for the warp and weft, Pascal's calculator, and Charles Babbage's difference engine are emblematic of an era of numerically coded machines. This period is also significant for the development of an increased mathematical understanding of the world, most significantly in the derivation of thermodynamics in the nineteenth century. As one of many transformative applications, a thermodynamic understanding of the world resulted in numerically quantified material properties.

As this theoretical body of knowledge transferred to material practices, most early efforts to quantify materials into a science were not of civilian or industrial origin but rather the product of military enterprise. The regularization of material properties and fabrication methods in particular was a matter of national security. Military enterprise is the area of production from whence the most consequential numerical control developments emerged.

United States Army Ordnance Department
In the nineteenth-century U.S. Army Ordnance Department, matter itself was increasingly engineered and controlled by numbers. Following victory in the War of 1812, the Ordnance Department redirected its efforts away from merely storing munitions to developing consistent fabrication processes and materials that would produce

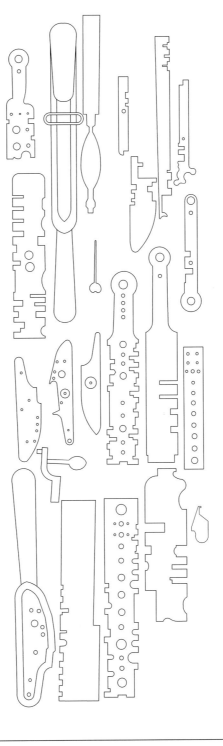

Fig.2 / Ordnance Department inspection gauges for Mississippi Rifle model 1841, by Eli Whitney Jr.

interchangeable components for firearms.[9] To standardize its practices, the Ordnance Department produced master jigs and material specifications that could control the production of weaponry in factories throughout the United States. They strategically decentralized the production process by regularizing the materials and methods of geographically distinct production sites through an elaborate command-and-control-style bureaucracy using railroads for physical transfer and telegraphs for information transfer. [Fig.2]

The research and production methods of the Ordnance Department prepared the development of numerical control in the twentieth century in a variety of important ways. First, the Ordnance Department was an early production system that regularized by a broad bureaucratic organization controlled with a network of unified materials, jig part patterns, and communication of information. Consequently, by the turn of the twentieth century, individuals from the Ordnance Department and the U.S. Army Corp of Engineers would develop the "American System of Management and Manufacture," commonly known as scientific management.[10] Second, the Ordnance Department's research on the metallurgy of the cannon, the rifle, and the conoidal bullet helped systematize material science in the United States. As such, the Ordnance Department advanced engineering design and training in the United States to its current practice.[11] This midcentury material science and engineering effort eventually engendered the innovative metallurgical basis for novel architectural practices during the late nineteenth century. Examples of this are works by James Bogardus and William Le Baron Jenney. Third, the switch from idiosyncratic craft-based production to standardized numerically controlled production in the Ordnance factories resulted in significant labor disputes, a recurrent theme when implementing numerically controlled fabrication techniques.

Finally, and perhaps most significantly, the funding structure of the U.S. Ordnance Department was an early expression of a permanent war economy. This funding model is characterized by the confluence of capital, security, research, and military enterprise. In this model, research, development, and trade relate not to the market but instead to defense expenditure.[12] The notion of permanent war for permanent peace fueled the search for new tactics and technology

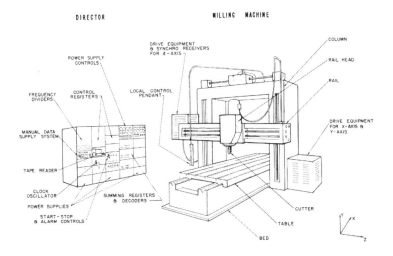

Fig. 3 / Conceptual layout of the experimental numerically controlled milling machine

during the nineteenth and twentieth centuries in the United States. By the twentieth century, battles were won and lost in offices, factories, and research facilities as much as on the battlefield.[13] In these technical, social, and economic domains, the nineteenth-century U.S. Army Ordnance Department was a mechanical rehearsal of the electronic numerical control techniques and technologies developed in the middle of the twentieth century. [Fig. 3]

Electronic Numerical Control

In the escalating arms race during the cold war, the Air Force developed a set of specifications for a manufacturing process that involved the consistent production of machined components for use in fighter planes and other weapon systems.[14] Lucrative contracts from the U.S. Department of Defense sponsored a vast research and development program. Initially the Servomechanisms Laboratory at the Massachusetts Institute of Technology (MIT) and a commercial helicopter rotary blade manufacturer received a contract and developed the Numerical Control Servo-System that is the basis for contemporary CAD and CAM systems.[15] This hardware and software system had the following notable developments: the use of the first computer-aided drafting program (the "Kludge"); the first intercontinental-networked design and production practice; and the first numerically controlled milling machines. Both computer-aided design and drafting (CADD) and parametric modeling were products of this enterprise. The Servomechanisms Laboratory's Kludge system became the basis of CADD software. The logic of the graphic display and the mouse-based input had its origins in this work. The development of solid modeling and parametric design in the French/British design of the Concorde aircraft is another example of trickle-down technology from aeronautical enterprise. The refinement and decreasing capital cost of such software and computer-controlled milling machines have lead to the eventual adoption of these techniques and technologies in architecture. By this point in this history of technology and design, it is apparent that military enterprise is the only real avant-garde practice in the United States. [Fig.4]

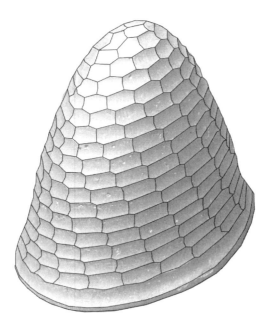

Fig. 4 / Drawing of a rough elliptical parabolical cut using the APT-III numerical control programming language, material unknown

The primary objective of the Air Force initiative was to automate the production process. The system was perfectly rational to the Air Force. Information for interchangeable components, designed in one location, could be stored on data tapes and sent to production, an electronic application of the mechanical command-and-control and the jig-based system of the Ordnance Department a century prior. In this process, the Air Force dreamt of fully automated factory floors, constantly producing complex components. This system claimed to shorten the loop between design and production. Management communicated directly with the machine, therefore commanding it. Hardly neutral, this conceptual direction taken by the Air Force—the fully automated factory floor—had two fundamental social and economic characteristics that affected its use in adjacent industries in America.

To achieve the perfect uniformity and repetition of machined parts, the production process had to reduce, if not eliminate, all variables from the material to the human. There was an overt ambition to eliminate the error and demands of a human technician and replace them with computer-driven machines. Straining against this dream were the realities of production and the variables of matter. One example of the difference between the theory and the practice was manifest in the 1960s when General Electric outfitted a Massachusetts factory with fully automated numerically controlled production. Since the capital-intensive infrastructure made the skilled machinist conceptually obsolete, General Electric dismissed most of its production staff and lowered the pay of those who remained. General Electric experienced 90 percent wasted part runs. This resulted in a socially and economically expensive situation, where General Electric eventually rehired its former staff and replaced the numerical control hardware and software. The issue is that the world of the machine and matter is not as rational as the Air Force dreamt it would be by implementing its numerically controlled vision of production. A General Electric machinist explains:

> The problem is that there are a lot of subtle things in drilling a hole.
> All you can tell a machine is that you start to drill at this point, you
> go in this deep, and you come back. But you can't tell a machine
> that there is a hard spot in this piece of metal it should push though

gently or if it starts overheating it has to back out. To change a tool, essentially you're taking a round peg and putting it in a round hole. It seems like a real simple thing. But if you actually analyze what was taking place with your muscles and nerve synapses, it's really pretty complicated. When you try and do this with a machine you have to have a hydraulic pump and all kinds of valves and switches, which can all break down.[16]

Alongside the history of numerical control runs a parallel history of labor and production. In the period of numerical control described above, labor shifts from human production to tool production and then from the tool to the program. This is a process which aims to automate machine production with minimal human interaction. Directly associated with this technical progression is a digression in the required knowledge and skill required of human labor. In each of these developments, numerical control alters the role of human judgment, skill, self-reliance, initiative, and creativity.[17] Most often, this atrophy diminishes the value and the wage of labor itself. One of its more acute effects is the displacement of work. This results in structural unemployment, an effect papably felt during the late 1970s and early '80s when factory production in the automotive industry transferred to automated production, sinking much of the upper Midwest into an economic depression while losing its skill base. Northern Europe and Japan, on the other hand, pursued an alternative model during this same period. They specified a hybrid system that still relied upon the technician's intelligence and skill, while automating certain aspects of production. This was a more socially and economically sustainable endeavor.[18] In contrast the American approach to numerically controlled technology was characterized by a cycle of rhetorical promises and technological transfer. There is often a vicious cycle of technological recurrence, where the failures and flaws of a previous technical system sanction yet another technical system to amend production. This is what David Noble describes as a "machine mentality," which, in his words, is the "understandable perhaps but nevertheless self-serving belief that whatever the problem, a machine is the solution. This manifests itself in a preference for, and tireless promotion of, capital-intensive methods and in the widespread but mistaken belief that the more capital intensive the process of production, the higher the productivity."[19]

Today a shift to wet digital fabrication processes from dry processes characterizes the trajectory of digital fabrication modes. Fluid-based fabrication eliminates some of the resistance that strained against the fully automated factory floor. Large-scale fabrication bureaus, such as RedEye ARC, have developed business and infrastructure models that can absorb the capital-intensive nature of this mode of fabrication. Others, such as Behrokh Khoshnevis, use numerically controlled wet construction to envision full-scale buildings rather than components. This is a more radical transformation of building technique than a simple substitution of digital for mechanical techniques. Such approaches carry yet another set of implications for the building industry, design, and society.

Digital Fabrication and Optimization

In each historical development of numerical control described above, the entities that have optimized and benefited the most from the numerically controlled techniques of standardization and automation have been large corporations and military enterprises with substantial capital initiatives and subsidized market structures. In each instance since the Industrial Revolution, the techniques that advance forms of numerically controlled fabrication have done so outside the market economy in which architects practice. Many government projects such as the Army Ordnance Department, the U.S. Navy's attempt at assembly line production during World War I with Henry Ford, the U.S. Air Force computer numerically controlled (CNC) program, and the NASA space exploration program, relied on immense federal funding.[20] Numerically controlled digital fabrication appliances were developed, and in the future they will only be optimized in context of massive capital investment. Such investment is not normally possible within the U.S. market economy; it is only possible with heavy government subsidies, as is the case of our military industrial complex. Similar to Noble's comments on the history of automated design and fabrication in the automobile industry, the "investigation of the actual design and use of capital-intensive, labor-saving, skill-reducing technology has begun to indicate that cost reduction was not a prime motivation, nor was it achieved."[21] He notes further: "If the primary motivations behind capital-intensive production methods were not necessarily economic, neither were the results."[22]

As this digital fabrication technology developed and has been slowly incorporated in architecture, a number of arguments point to numerically controlled production practices in other industries such the aerospace or ship-building industries.[23] Such arguments question why architecture has not developed production techniques in parallel progressions. The primary answer is simple and powerful: architecture engages a vastly different market structure and must negotiate a more varied set of demands. Capital-intensive enterprises and economies of scale are fundamental economic principles of standardization and automation, and these principles are fundamentally at odds with aspects of architectural practice, including the customization of building types for particular codes, sites, budgets, performances, and preferences.

In architecture, digital fabrication technologies will not change building production without fundamental shifts in the social and market structures of design practice. For example, the most significant transformation of Frank Gehry's practice was not a range of digital techniques and technologies adopted by practice in the 1990s; rather it was modifications to his contract structure that engendered the techniques and technologies of their work, a social—rather than technical—implement.[24] Thus, what works for Gehry Partners may not work for other architectural practices with fundamentally different fee structures. Architecture lacks most often the economies of scale, massive capital, and government subsidies that optimize these technologies in adjacent disciplines, no matter how much we rhetorically compare our industry to others. Further, the need for customization in architecture, though possible in digital fabrication, strains against the uniformity stressed throughout the history of numerical control. These historical factors condition the application of digital fabrication in architecture. The course of these histories can be swerved to complement architectural agendas, though this requires a grasp of the historical and social substrate that enabled digital fabrication.

Numerical control is just that: it is a set of techniques for controlling numbers. Yet, in all of the above cases, the technical benefits of military technologies are not the only effects of the technology transfer process. Technology transfer also transfers a set of inseparable social effects. These effects are as real as any CNC-milled object. Each instance of standardization and automation are rehearsals of the implementation for successive technologies such as digital fabrication. In each case, the habits of mind and processes that engendered the previous technology extend into the next; a recurrent pattern of thoughts and decisions are evident in the promotion, marketing, argumentation, and implementation of successive techniques.

Standardizing and automating numerical control techniques does not prescribe an automatic and standardized future. A series of social decisions and habits determine the course of these techniques. This draws attention to the role of technology in architecture—in this case digital fabrication technologies—not as a technically determined practice, but rather one that evolves over time and is itself determined though social and cultural needs and developments. Architecture has historically been too willing to promote the capabilities of technologies while ignoring the culpabilities. With each successive wave of new technologies, architects seem to lose more ground than they gain. In this receding horizon of practice our hasty rush toward perpetual novelty neglects to study the technologies that we enthusiastically grant such great momentum. This suggests, even demands, an alternate way for designers to understand, practice, and implement technology. As technology comes to dominate our lives and practices, architects must deepen their engagement with it, not as automated technocrats solving isolated problems, but as mindful participants in our technical practices and the systemic assemblage of its multivariate parameters. If there will be a paradigm shift in architecture, it will occur in the complexity of the social rather than the technical field. As David Noble noted, "There are no technological promises, only human ones, and social progress must not be reduced to, or confused with, mere technological progress."[25]

Kiel Moe is an architect and assistant professor of architecture at Northeastern University, and is the author of *Integrated Design in Contemporary Architecture* and *Thermally Active Surfaces in Architecture*, both from Princeton Architectural Press.

Notes

1 Gilles Deleuze and Claire Parnet, *Dialogues II* (New York: Columbia University Press, 1987), 70.

2 V. Gordon Childe, "Rotary Motion," in *A History of Technology, Volume 1: From Early Times to Fall of Ancient Empires*, ed. Charles Singer, E. J. Holland, and A. R. Hall (New York: Oxford University Press, 1955), 187–215. In this volume, Harrison and Childe provide an excellent account of the partial rotary and full rotary motion tools for drilling and fire making in the archaic world.

3 H. S. Harrison, "Fire-Making, Fuel, and Lighting," in *A History of Technology, Volume 1*, 220–30.

4 J. Francis Reintjes, *Numerical Control: Making a New Technology* (New York: Oxford University Press, 1991).

5 Lewis Mumford, *Technics and Civilization* (New York: Harcourt Brace & Company, 1963).

6 Ibid., 9–59. Lewis Mumford focused on this technique in the chapter "Cultural Preparation," which looks at the series of developments related to the clock as well as those in these adjacent practices.

7 Ibid, 12–22.

8 Bill Addis, *Building: 3000 Years of Design, Engineering, and Construction* (London: Phaidon Press, 2007), 169.

9 Merrit Roe Smith, ed., "Army Ordnance and the 'American System' of Manufacturing," *Military Enterprise and Technological Change: Perspective on the American Experience* (Cambridge, MA: MIT Press, 1985), 39–86.

10 Ibid., introduction, 12–15. Charles F. O'Connell Jr.'s account of the railroad development and the development of the American style of management is also relevant here. Charles F. O'Connell Jr., "The Corp of Engineers and the Rise of Modern Management, 1827–1856," in *Military Enterprise and Technological Change*, 87–116.

11 David F. Noble, *America by Design: Science, Technology, and the Rise of Capitalism* (Oxford: Oxford University Press, 1977).

12 Seymour Melman, *The Permanent War Economy: American Capitalism in Decline* (New York: Simon and Schuster, 1974).

13 Alex F. Osborn, *The Optimism Book for Offices: How to Standardize and Systematize to Meet War-Created Business Problems* (Jamestown, NY: Art Metal Construction Co., 1918). This book provides an excellent period source for the mental habits of the relationship between war and industry at the end of World War I.

14 J. Francis Retijles, *Numerical Control*, 134–40.

15 Ibid., 141–63.

16 David F. Noble, *Forces of Production: A Social History of Industrial Automation* (New York: Alfred A. Knopf, 1984), 345–46.

17 Ibid., 265–323. The chapter "Who's Running the Shop" focuses on the designed utopia and actual conditions of fully automated production and the increase of labor rather than decrease in labor, a theme throughout the book.

18 Ibid., 145–92. This chapter, "The Road Not Taken," focuses on the alternatives to fully automated production methods. He shows that some of these alternatives were adapted by Japanese and European counterparts and demonstrates how the alternatives provide a more supple system of production with fewer economical and social challenges.

19 David F. Noble, "Statement of David F. Noble at Hearings on Industrial Sub-Committee of the 98th U.S. Congress," *Progress Without People* (Chicago: Charles H. Kerr Publishing, 1993), 100.

20 David F. Noble, "Command and Performance: A Perspective on Military Enterprise and Technological Change," in *Military Enterprise and Technological Change*, 329–46.

21 Ibid., 334

22 Ibid., 335.

23 Stephan Kieran and James Timberlake, *Refabricating Architecture: How Manufacturing Methodologies are Poised to Transform Building Construction* (New York: McGraw-Hill, 2003), xi.

24 Carl Sapers, "Towards Architectural Practice in the 21st Century: The Demise (and Rebirth?) of Professionalism," *Harvard Design Magazine* 19 (2003–2004 Fall–Winter): 80–85.

25 Noble, *Forces of Production*, 351.

ON SHELLS AND BLOBS: STRUCTURAL SURFACES IN THE DIGITAL AGE

Martin Bechthold

In this essay, Martin Bechthold addresses the lack of structural sophistication in much contemporary "blob" architecture and argues for the investigation of promising predigital research in structurally efficient thin-shell curved systems in order to fully realize the untapped potential of intelligent digital design and manufacturing technologies.

We all know that computer-aided design and manufacturing (CAD/CAM) technology has triggered a proliferation of complexly shaped building designs, including the free forms we call "blobs." But we have forgotten that many of these fluid shapes resemble concrete roof shells that appeared in the first half of the twentieth century—shells devised to cover long spans with a minimum of material. There is, of course, a difference, and it hinges on structure.

It is often assumed that all curved surfaces are necessarily stiff and thus useful as primary structural elements. [Fig.1] Surface curvature, however, forms a structurally effective shell only if it enables efficient membrane stresses to develop, which in turn allow thin surfaces to carry significant loads. This structural elegance contrasts with

Fig. 1 / Disney Concert Hall, Gehry Partners, Los Angeles, California, 2002

the relative clumsiness of the support systems for digitally generated irregular shapes.

It is true that shells cannot offer the degree of formal freedom for building skins and roofs that blobs offer, but why, given their compensating efficient use of material, are they practically forgotten amidst the frenzy about blobs? Architecture schools generally offer digital design classes, but hardly any schools address the design of structural surfaces.[1] This disinterest in shells dates back to the early 1980s and reflects an avoidance of the immense constructional challenges that these systems pose. But can CAD/CAM technology make the construction of material-efficient structural surfaces easier? Can digital technology not only assist in expanding formal design, but also enable the use of material-efficient structural systems?

With current discourse focusing on the underlying shaping principles of "digital architecture," architects often overlook the fact that the formal complexity of the blob is achieved through conventional constructional and structural means—skeletons assembled from linear and curvilinear members that support secondary members and nonstructural building skins.[2] [Fig. 2] These systems rely heavily on bending

Fig. 2 / Detail of canopy supports, Disney Concert Hall, Gehry Partners, Los Angeles, California, 2002

stresses—the least efficient of the basic load-carrying methods. The visible surface of the free-form shape is structurally functionless. The curvature present in free-form shapes rarely allows membrane stresses to develop, since the underlying shaping algorithms are optimized for visualization purposes and cannot accurately simulate and model structural behavior. These shapes leave little choice other than those structural systems that rely on inefficient bending action. The in-plane membrane stresses of the shell are vastly more efficient: less material is needed to carry comparable loads.

Structurally efficient shells use construction technology that has progressed only marginally since the 1980s. This stagnation in technology contrasts starkly with the significant advances in digital design and manufacturing systems for skeletal structures. Steel detailing software and the related computer numerical control (CNC) manufacturing facilities partially automate the design and fabrication of structural members of skeletal frames, including the complex support systems of free-form shapes. Now new computer-driven manufacturing technology is needed for shell construction if this material-efficient system is to become a viable alternative.

The development in the 1920s of structural roof shells stemmed from a fascination with a new material—reinforced concrete—and the need to cover medium to large spans economically. Felix Candela in Mexico, Eduardo Torroja in Spain, Eladio Dieste in Uruguay, Franz Dischinger and Ulrich Finsterwalder in Germany, Heinz Isler in Switzerland, and Anton Tedesco in the United States were among the pioneer shell builders. The labor-intensive construction of the complex shape was economically justified through significant savings in materials: Candela's shell for a restaurant in Xochimilco, Mexico, (1958) spans 106 feet (32.3 meters) with concrete just 1.7 inches (4.3 centimeters) thick.

Concrete shells include single-curved shapes such as cylinders and cones, as well as a variety of double-curved geometries. Double-curvature synclastic (with curves running in same direction) and anticlastic (with curves running in opposite directions) shapes are structurally particularly efficient, but the construction of their formwork is technically more demanding. Hyperbolic paraboloids (HP) and hyperboloids form a particular group within anticlastic shells. They combine an efficient load-bearing mechanism with relative ease of construction: the formwork for these surfaces can be made mostly from straight wooden boards. The majority of Candela's concrete shells—as well as some timber shells by other designers—are based on HP shapes.

Early shell builders employed simple geometries that could easily be geometrically described and built.[3] Heinz Isler developed a new concept for shells in the 1950s by deriving shell geometry from experiments with accurate physical models such as inflatable rubber membranes or hanging fabric. These shells are equilibrium shapes—their shapes balance loads such as the weight of the shell through membrane stresses. Also in the '50s, researchers at Frei Otto's Institute of Lightweight Construction at the University of Stuttgart experimented with form-finding methods for tensile systems by studying minimal surfaces using soap bubbles. Their physical models were later complemented and partially replaced by computational form-finding methods, applicable to both tensile systems and shells. Designing an equilibrium shell means defining a structurally efficient shape through the specification of its support conditions and loads. Each prescribed combination of support and load will yield a unique geometry.

The advances in computational form-finding of the 1970s came at a time when the interest in shells was rapidly fading. Fabric structures, cable nets, and space frames (triangulated bar networks) presented equally efficient structural solutions for spanning larger distances, but their constructional problems were more readily solved with the established building technology for skeletal structures. The few shells built after the 1970s were mostly grid shells, with the continuous surface replaced by linear or curvilinear interconnected members.

What are the current technical impediments to shell construction? The making of a complexly shaped surface is necessarily challenging, even more so if this surface becomes the primary structural element. Common shaping or forming techniques may be applicable to thin materials such as sheet metal or wooden boards, but these elements by themselves are insufficient for roof shells. Shell construction techniques have traditionally relied heavily on labor, and consequently are hampered by today's high labor costs. Labor costs (not adjusted for inflation) between 1958 and 2002 increased between factors of eight (unskilled labor) and eleven (manufacturing labor), whereas the cost of construction materials (not adjusted for inflation) increased during the same time period only by factors between 3.8 (steel milled products) and 4.8 (ready-mixed concrete).[4] Less labor-intensive construction techniques need to be devised if shell construction is to become feasible today. Formwork accounts for a major part of the cost of concrete shells, and only by reusing these expensive, large molds can shells be economical. Heinz Isler, one of the few remaining active shell builders, reuses formwork in different projects, accepting the severe design restriction to regular plan geometries, the repetition of identical shapes, and the inability to adjust to local conditions.

Research at the Harvard University Graduate School of Design has been suggesting new processes for shell construction using CAD/CAM technology. The accuracy of CNC fabrication now enables the subdivision of larger shells into panels that can be prefabricated, transported to sites, and assembled into larger roof shells. Researchers are developing and prototyping three types: a laminated-timber sandwich shell, a ferro-cement folded plate system with thin cement slabs reinforced by steel mesh, and a concrete shell system constructed with prefabricated "lost" formwork that becomes embedded in the structure.

The timber shell is a rigid sandwich with a high-density foam core and laminated wood facings. The foam core of individual panels can be fabricated on a CNC-milling machine. Multiple layers of precut strips of sliced thick veneer or plywood are then laminated over the surface and cured under vacuum pressure. Specially engineered lap or finger joints connect individual panels and form the shell. The sandwich can be designed to satisfy current thermal insulation requirements, fire-resistance, and structural rigidity. The depth of the overall system is sufficient to embed service elements, thus further enhancing multifunctionality in the geometrically complex roof. The sandwich, in combination with certain core and facing materials, can generate enough stiffness to accommodate moderate bending stresses. Not only shells, but also free-form shapes can be manufactured according to this method, as long as the bending stiffness of the sandwich suffices. At last the shell catches up with the blob: a technology developed for structural surfaces can be a viable alternative to the skeletal construction of free-form shapes.[5]

The ferro-cement folded plate system revisits both a forgotten system and an exciting material no longer used in industrialized countries. Folded plates are closely related to shells, because their load-bearing mechanism is principally derived from the in-plane stresses of a thin folded surface.[6] The constructional problems of folded plates are the relative complexity of formwork in concrete systems and the difficulty of creating efficient connections between flat panels in timber systems. An obvious solution is to use a material that combines stiffness and a capability for folding without relying on elaborate on-site formwork: thin sheets of a mesh-reinforced composite—ferro-cement.[7] Ferro-cement panels can be manufactured efficiently on flat, reusable formwork. Predetermined fold lines are not covered with mortar during this process—these lines effectively act as hinges in the folding process. Here the steel reinforcing mesh yields on bending, and flat concrete plates can be folded like origami into a three-dimensional structure.

The open joints are covered with mortar after the folding. Based on a 1980 Australian patent application, this concept has not yet been pursued beyond small-scale experiments carried out at the University of Sydney.[8]

CAD/CAM technology streamlines the design-to-production process. Complex folded systems are generated digitally, and integrated structural analysis tools provide rapid feedback on the feasibility of schemes. The components of the design models are then digitally flattened into 2-D production patterns that are produced on CNC lasers or routers. The reinforced panels are fabricated through either manual or partially automated spraying of the mortar over the reinforcing mesh. The folds have to be carefully engineered, and excessive bending of the plates needs to be avoided during folding.[9] A wide range of custom shapes can be produced by this method: the number of individually shaped panels in a project has little impact on manufacturing time and costs. Parametric variations of a folded-plate system—inherently simple to generate using design development software such as SolidWorks or CATIA—can be manufactured and assembled more efficiently than they could be using traditional on-site construction techniques.

A third research investigation is developing a system of shaped ferro-cement panels to be used on-site as lost formwork for a load-bearing layer of cast-in-place concrete and reinforcement. This approach—closely related to Pier Luigi Nervi's use of lost formwork in the 1950s and '60s—specifically addresses the need for reduced formwork cost by making the formwork a structural part of the finished shell. The ferro-cement elements are manufactured accurately off-site using CNC machines and spraying of mortar that may be partially automated. Overlapping reinforcement bars that become embedded in the cast-in-place concrete secure structural connections between adjacent panels in the finished shell.[10]

These three processes for the design and production of individualized and material-efficient structural surfaces use CAD/CAM technology to allow architects greater variety of shapes while reducing the additional cost normally associated with customized construction. The problem of having to employ identical elements repetitively is, however, not limited to shells; it is a part of much building construction.

The use of standard products and components is a generally accepted design imperative. Everyday construction products—from plywood and standard steel shapes to suspended ceiling systems and light fixtures—come in few variations. The building industry operates largely under economic principles that originate in the laws of early industrial mass production, and the customization of products usually implies significant cost increases. Will CAD/CAM eliminate the need for repetition altogether, thus drastically affecting the way we design?

The possibility of thoroughly customized buildings with individualized components is attractive to architects. "Mass customization" has enabled the production of individualized products in other industries at a price similar to that of equivalent mass-produced items. Mass-customized products range from customized books to individualized machines for industrial production. The building industry has been adapting to this trend: individualized windows are now designed online, and the components are usually manufactured automatically. Walls are constructed using sets of prefabricated building blocks that are designed, CNC cut, and delivered to sites "just in time," increasing construction speed and reducing waste. This incremental implementation of mass customization in the building industry has hardly been noticed. It is likely that we will continue to use standard products and materials in buildings, but interesting opportunities for designers, engineers, and contractors may arise where they are least expected. A recent example is the manufacture of custom steel reinforcement mats for concrete slabs—digitally designed and robotically welded—that can save a substantial percentage of steel because each mat is precisely tailored to the stresses and deflections present in the slab.

What objective can, or rather, *should* customization serve? The study of shells demonstrates that it may enable structurally efficient construction systems, provide a rich spatial experience, and use material resources responsibly. Customization through CAD/CAM could and should be directed toward a more efficient response to performance requirements as diverse as program, structure, energy efficiency, lighting, and maintenance. Digital technology is not an end in itself but should play a role in creating a more human, socially responsible, and sustainable environment. Before long, today's separate discourses on sustainability and digital design will, we can assume, productively connect.

Martin Bechthold is an architect and professor of architectural technology at the Harvard University Graduate School of Design. He is author of numerous essays and books including *Innovative Surface Structures*.

Notes

1 In April 2003, I conducted a survey of courses offered at nineteen major American architectural schools. Occasionally shells were briefly mentioned in survey structures courses. My course at the Harvard Graduate School of Design was the only one to cover shells in any depth. The schools included in the survey are Yale, Princeton, Cornell, the University of California at Berkeley, MIT, UCLA, the University of Colorado at Bolder, the University of Florida, Georgia Institute of Technology, IIT, Tulane, the University of Michigan, Columbia, Rhode Island School of Design, the State University of New York at Buffalo, Rensselaer, and the University of Texas at Austin.

2 See for example *Journal of Architectural Education*, November 2002, and many recent books and publications.

3 German engineers pursued a complete quantitative understanding of simple cylindrical shells prior to building prototypes. Candela's more daring HP shapes were often built without complete theoretical understanding of their structural behavior—Candela has referred to his workers as the ones that solved many technical problems directly on-site. Thomas Herzog and Jose-Luis Moro's interview with Felix Candela in "Zum Werk von Felix Candela," ARCUS 18 (1992): 10–22.

4 Samuel H. Williamson, "The Relative Cost of Unskilled Labor in the United States, 1774–present," *Economic History Services*, March 2003, http://www.eh.net/hmit/unskilledlabor, accessed 2003. U.S. Department of Labor, Bureau of Labor Statistics.

5 See Martin Bechthold, "Complex Shapes in Wood: Computer Aided Design and Manufacturing Techniques," (PhD diss., Harvard University, 2001).

6 A recent folded-plate structure, albeit a hybrid through a combination with trusses, is the roof of the Yokohama International Port Terminal (2002) by Foreign Office Architects.

7 Joseph-Louis Lambot in France invented ferro-cement in 1848, a year before Joseph Monier's use of reinforced concrete. Ferro-cement features excellent crack control due to the large bonding surface between the mesh layers and the matrix. It is extremely versatile and has been successfully used for an extremely wide range of applications, from seagoing vessels and water tanks to prefabricated housing panels and medium-span roof systems.

8 In 1980 two lecturers in Civil Engineering at the University of Sydney, Wheen and Jackson, applied for a patent on the bending of ferro-cement slabs. R. J. Wheen and G. N. Jackson, "Method of Bending Hardened and Stiff Slabs," Australian Patent Application No. PE 3167, April 1980.

9 My team and I used a comparatively simple folded-plate system to develop a hinge detailing strategy and the folding apparatus. The process was then tested on a six-foot-long prototype.

10 These ongoing research projects are conducted at and funded by the Harvard University Graduate School of Design. Team members include Jerome Chang, Jason Halaby, Chung-Ping Lee, Mark Oldham, Tyrone Yang, and me.

DIMINISHING DIFFICULTY: MASS CUSTOMIZATION AND THE DIGITAL PRODUCTION OF ARCHITECTURE

Dan Willis and Todd Woodward

In this concluding essay, authors Dan Willis and Todd Woodward critically respond to widespread claims about the industry-changing potential of digital fabrication and mass customization, taking particular aim at Stephen Kieran and James Timberlake's book Refabricating Architecture: How Manufacturing Methodologies are Poised to Transform Building Construction. *This essay clearly situates* Refabricating Architecture *within the context of architectural debates of the last two decades and provides an excellent discussion of the emergence of digital technologies in architectural practice, spanning from the 1980s introduction of computer aided design (CAD) to today's much heralded "digital revolution."*

Towards a Newer Architecture
You probably recall the succinct advice offered to Dustin Hoffman in *The Graduate* by an inebriated party guest: "Plastics." Should a recent college graduate, intending to pursue a masters degree in architecture,

encounter a similar know-it-all today, a single word of advice would no longer suffice. Assuming the would-be mentor actually knew something about the state of architectural practice, the two-word phrase would be "mass customization."

Mass customization, in the words of Stephen Kieran and James Timberlake, "proposes new processes to build using automated production, but with the ability to differentiate each artifact from those fabricated before and after."[1] Mass customization and digital fabrication are hot topics in architecture offices, magazines, and schools. Architecture departments in many universities now own or have access to laser and waterjet cutters, rapid-prototyping equipment, computer numerically controlled (CNC) milling machines, routers, and cutters. The most recent conference of the Association for Computer Aided Design in Architecture (ACADIA) was devoted to digital fabrication, as was the cover story in the June 2004 issue of *Architecture* magazine.[2]

Kieran and Timberlake, prominent Philadelphia-based architects, received a Benjamin Latrobe Research Fellowship in 2001 to study what they termed "transfer technologies"—manufacturing methodologies in other fields that could be applied to building construction. The study resulted in their popular *Refabricating Architecture* (2004), which encourages architects to adopt "information-based" design and production techniques from other industries. The book is self-consciously modeled on Le Corbusier's *Towards a New Architecture.* The authors' message is clear—architecture is beginning its next revolution.

The migration of interest in these topics from the architectural subculture of computer-savvy "geeks" to the mainstream of the profession was sparked by the positive reception of Frank Gehry's Guggenheim Museum Bilbao (1997). The media coverage of this project introduced architects to the CATIA software Gehry's office employed and championed the idea that Gehry's practice was bridging the barrier between design and fabrication, returning the architect to a master-builder role. Gehry claimed that his computerized working methods were "a way for me to get closer to the craft," and that, as his office is using it, "the computer is not dehumanizing; it's an interpreter."[3] On the heels of Gehry's titanium undulations came "Blob Architecture," popularized by Gregg Lynn's *Animate Form* (1999).[4]

Gehry's design process, with a sketch leading to a physical study model leading to a digital model, and Lynn's blobs, which initially represent forces, influences, and performance characteristics but not necessarily building shapes, are not the revolution *Refabricating Architecture* has in mind, but they are its precursors. Before an "IT [information technology] Revolution" could occur in the architecture profession, practicing architects had to see built examples—actual buildings realized using digital technologies—that went beyond computer drafting, and architecture students had to see computer technologies facilitating the work of the visionary designers they respected.[5]

A Brief History

Prior to the late 1990s, architects—unlike, for example, industrial designers—had embraced computer-aided design (CAD) but not computer-aided manufacturing (CAM). More than a decade earlier, architects began using computers in ways that imitated the manual typing, bookkeeping, and drafting procedures customary to the profession. While CAD changed the way most architects created construction drawings, it did not immediately change the role of these drawings in the production of buildings. Early CAD programs actually borrowed many of their features—drawings that were composed of multiple layers for instance—from "systems drafting" techniques that predated computerized drafting.[6] The substitution of hand-drafting techniques with computer-based alternatives still accounts for most computer use by practicing architects. Outside the academy, this shift in means of drawing production has gone largely unquestioned, and is seen as an inevitable result of advancing technology and the need to increase productivity.

CAD programs originally processed only two-dimensional drawing and were therefore primarily useful for construction documentation. During the 1990s, architects and architectural educators focused their attention on ways to more completely represent buildings and environments. *Virtual reality* was the phrase of that decade. Faster computers and improving software allowed architects to create increasingly realistic virtual environments, often explored through animated "walk-throughs" or sophisticated interactive devices allowing viewers to control their movements through virtual space. Although animations have proven useful for presentation purposes, virtual reality tools were initially and primarily intended to help architects *design*. With the exception of cases in which the virtual environments were themselves an end product, such as for the video game industry, these developments in visualization had little direct connection to creating real buildings and building components.

Even today, a "digital divide" between construction documentation and advanced visual representation persists in most architecture practices. Architecture firms often use both 2-D and 3-D software in the course of a project, with "designers" using a modeling program, such as form-Z or Autodesk VIZ, to design the building, while the "production" staff creates working drawings using AutoCAD or a similar software. Although some integration of 2-D- and 3-D-software packages has been possible for a while, these two means of representing buildings have remained largely separate in practice.

Where We Are Today

Recent software advances promise more: to fully integrate 2-D and 3-D computer representation and to attach meaningful specification information to all elements in the computer representation of a building.[7] For various reasons, attempts to create such "smart drawings" have so far failed to take hold in the profession. As currently practiced in most offices, embedding drawings with detailed engineering and quality control specifications and later extracting that information has proven tedious. As Branko Kolarevic, one of the primary chroniclers of the state of architectural computing, notes, the problem is more "cultural than technological."[8] Most architecture firms still find the old "dumb" drawings, combined with separate written specifications, to be the most reliable way to produce construction documentation. There are significant risks for the "early adopters" of a new project delivery method.[9] Although the American Institute of Architects (AIA) now has a task force working on these issues, important legal aspects of practice, such as ownership of documents, professional liability, and use of the architect's design by others, remain mired in predigital conventions.[10] However, the vision is of a means of representation that promises coordination during design, fewer errors during construction documentation, and ease of translation into a constructed building. The architect's computer model will become a complete virtual building, without ambiguity, and will anticipate each component of the actual building, no matter how small. The perfectly accurate computer model paves the way for the perfect translation, by way of digital fabrication and mass customization, of the architect's intentions into the physical building. Here is the anticipation of revolution.

Revolutions, however, are notoriously difficult to predict. Whether the rapid developments in computer technologies and their applications in architectural practice are revolutionary or evolutionary is still unclear. A tendency for marketing to overshadow dispassionate analysis plagues discussions of information technology, even within the academy. This does not necessarily diminish the magnitude of the IT-fueled changes about to overtake architectural practice. Great as their effects may be, the predicted transformations all stem from three related advances: building information modeling, parametric modeling, and mass customization. Together, these three techniques are poised to significantly alter the ways professional architects work.

How these may come together to revolutionize architecture is summarized in Branko Kolarevic's compilation of essays, *Architecture in the Digital Age: Design and Manufacturing* (2003): "The currently separate professional realms of architecture, engineering, and construction can be integrated into a relatively seamless digital collaborative enterprise, in which architects could play a central role as *information master builders*, the twenty-first century version of the architect's medieval predecessors." According to Kolarevic, this new age is characterized by a "direct correlation between what can be designed and what can be built."[11] This claim implies that what Robin Evans termed the "translation from drawing to building" has been replaced by methods that make such translations unnecessary.[12] If indeed "constructability becomes a direct function of computability," as some predict, this will also mean that there is less and less adjustment of the architect's design in the field in response to material irregularities or site conditions.[13] The CONSTRUCTABILITY= COMPUTABILITY equation should in theory increase the architect's control over the project and make building costs more predictable.

However, it also renders the skilled building trades largely obsolete and reduces opportunities for taking advantage of serendipitous occurrences during construction, eliminating the sorts of chance happenings that artists, and many architects, often find enliven their works.

Building Information Modeling

While still not a dominant practice, building information modeling (BIM) is perhaps furthest along, among the three new techniques, in terms of general acceptance by the architecture profession and construction industry.[14] Using examples from the aerospace industry, Kieran and Timberlake encourage architects to accelerate their transition from the "representation" of buildings to something like the computer "simulation" of airplanes under construction. In the design of airplanes, each component is fully defined in the simulation, so that "any dimension can be derived completely and accurately from the solid model, rendering the once necessary dimensional drawings now obsolete."[15] Since BIM would transfer the same advantages, mainly greater completeness and accuracy, to building production, building information models may indeed be poised to replace CAD-generated construction drawings. If and when they do, there will be unprecedented demands for accuracy of the architect's computer modeling, but there may also be the potential for increased control over the built work.

Unlike the proverbial map so detailed that it was the size of the kingdom it depicted and therefore useless, a building information model can (in theory) embody the same amount of detail and complexity as the full-size building, but by virtue of its inherent scalelessness, it can be enlarged or reduced to reveal only the information needed at any one moment. According to architectural computing pioneer Charles Eastman, this should "finally allow the demise of architectural drawings as a contract of record for a building project."[16] Of course, the perfect BIM assumes that there are no errors or omissions in the architect's design. The BIM, through its very completeness, is supposed to make design mistakes less likely. Just as they are typically identified during construction, so should they be discovered as inconsistencies in the virtual building model.[17]

Modeling Imperfection

Interestingly, the virtual reality of the BIM is actually more precise than the material world. Bernard Cache describes the process of creating a digital model capable of accurately constructing a series of adjacent elements:

> But, as nothing in "real" reality is truly exact, and as the software is fully exact, we also had to define small gaps to account for "errors" in the production and assembly, such as adding the paint or varnish after machining, which can make the parts sufficiently thicker to introduce inaccuracies into the process.[18]

These artificially defined gaps, which facilitate the precise computer-controlled fabrication of building elements and allow for their assembly in an imprecise world, require the judgment of an architect or building expert. We believe the inevitable "errors" present in reality, including natural processes such as thermal expansion and weathering, make it impossible to achieve a *direct* correlation between digital data and a constructed building. Interpolation, based on an understanding of construction tolerances, material behavior, and the ergonomics of building assembly, will always be required.

Since a gap between the BIM and the building is inevitable and potentially advantageous, the question remaining is: how big a gap should there be? We predict that the appropriate gap will be determined by trial and error and will vary depending not only on the scale, but also on the intentions of the project. For example, custom houses, corporate headquarters, and other "signature" buildings will be modeled more accurately than ordinary commercial or residential buildings. Successful practices will become conventionalized and then established as standards of the profession. While the gap between the building and the model will continue to narrow, it will remain a potential site for the invention and imagination of the architect and craftsperson. As architects become more accustomed to working in this new way, it is likely that rapid-prototyping equipment and CNC-produced mockups will be more often used to verify particularly important details in the building's construction during the design phase. The physical mock-up will then allow architects to fine-tune the BIM and help ensure that construction tolerances and reality's imperfections are considered in the model.

BIM: Different, But Not That Different

The culture of building construction documentation must change if BIM is to become optimally useful. Many parts of the typical building project are simply never drawn according to the current conventions of 2-D construction drawings on paper. Electrical conduit runs, the exact routing of plumbing lines, communications and security system wiring, the precise pattern of joints in stone masonry, the location of shims and spacers—none of these appears on conventional construction drawings. These practices may, for good reason, prove resistant to change. In this case, we will have to accept a larger gap between the BIM and the building. The ease by which these aspects of construction can be modified at the building site may mean that the time spent to incorporate them into a BIM is not cost-effective, or is not recoverable by the architect. On the other hand, digital technologies may eventually allow far greater standardization and prefabrication of these building components now invisible on the drawings. Electrical wiring for buildings could, for instance, take on the characteristics of the modular circuits connected by wiring harnesses found in automobiles. Or, as clients discover that the BIM is the ideal facilities management tool—as useful after the building is constructed as before—they may be willing to pay a premium for fully detailed BIM. Rather than the notoriously inaccurate "as-built" drawings with which most facilities managers make do, BIMs can in theory mirror the physical building throughout its entire life cycle.

By calling the virtual buildings "models" or "simulations" rather than "drawings" or "representations," writers like Kieran and Timberlake try to distinguish the latest generation of digital building representations from earlier ones. This nomenclature obscures the fact that a building information model, just like the orthographic drawings it is intended to replace, is an abstract *projection* of a future building. The word *projection* captures both the forward-looking nature of these techniques and the fact that what is being represented is the Cartesian "extension" of the project.

Regardless of what sort of descriptive geometry the BIM uses, it will primarily represent the future building's *shape*. Even when specification information is embedded in the BIM, descriptions of the building's *qualities* will rely on text. This means that the BIM and the design tools that often precede it (such as form-finding parametric modeling techniques—see below) privilege some kinds of information over others in ways very similar to those that drawings employing descriptive geometries have always done. Simply put, a building's shape has always been comparatively easier to represent accurately than its other aspects, such as its significance in a society, its character, or even its material properties. This, we believe, has led to the architecture profession's historic overemphasis on building shapes at the expense of other, harder to define qualities—an overemphasis the latest digital techniques simply perpetuate.[19]

Most proponents of architecture's IT revolution would disagree. Kolarevic, for one, insists that what the latest computer-generated architecture looks like is of secondary importance to the ways it is designed and built. Kolarevic and others are correct to claim that digital technologies have become generative tools for architects, rather than merely a means of representing buildings. Though he makes this point sincerely in an effort to focus attention on the full potential of digital processes, he leaves unmentioned the role that the formal novelty of computer-generated "smooth architectures" plays in the media attention devoted to the handful of designers producing bloblike constructions. Like the modernist revolutionaries that preceded them, proponents of the digital revolution argue that the latest digitally enabled architecture is not a style. Although Kolarevic maintains that it is unimportant that digital design tools generate curved forms, he spends several pages and uses detailed mathematical definitions to discuss the modeling of curves made possible by parametric modeling software.[20] (Other architects blame the ubiquity of curves and blobs on the software, or mention the inability of most architects to program software to their liking.[21]) Most that is written about the latest computer-generated architecture repeats the old news that architects are importing technologies of production from the automobile, aerospace, and ship-building industries without questioning *why* the "smooth morphologies" characteristic of the shapes of these things (which, unlike buildings, move) are being imported as well.[22]

Parametric Modeling

Parametric modeling, or just "parametrics," is the second significant digital development affecting architectural practice. Parametric design processes require the designer to establish clear design goals and then manipulate various design parameters to achieve them. The parameters—usually mathematical descriptions of certain geometric relationships—are inputs the designer makes into a computer program that generate design alternatives.

> Parametric modeling is a way of defining geometry in which geometric dependencies are built in, so that editing one shape will cause the other shapes to change size or location. Thus, the general idea is to make certain design parameters *formulas*, rather than just numbers. The specific idea is to create a CAD model that encompasses design intent, not just a point design. For example, a hole that is supposed to be in the center of a face could be created that way with an equation, so that no matter how the face is resized, the hole always relocates itself to the center.[23]

Rather than beginning their design process by sketching ideas for a building's shape, designers can use parametrics to explore a wide variety of options that respond to subtle changes in the programmatic (in the usual architect's sense of the term) intentions for the project. "In parametric design, it is the parameters of a particular design that are declared, not its shape," Kolaravic writes.[24] As Eastman indicates, parametrics can be used to generate BIM, and there are efficiencies to be gained by doing so. Parametric software is intended to help designers handle "complex competing design constraints in an interactive way."[25]

Taken out of context, some of the claims for parametric modeling—such as Kolarevic's: "parametric design calls for the rejection of fixed solutions and for an exploration of infinitely variable potentialities"—might lead one to believe that parametrics can address any variable to which architecture might respond.[26]

But parametric design methods do both more and less than the graphic problem-solving and programming techniques—such as matrices, decision trees, and network diagrams—popular in the 1970s.[27] Like these earlier methods, parametrics attempt to make design decision-making more systematic, but do so by replacing the "intuitive design of variants [with] mathematical-mechanical strategies in the design phase to make it more efficient."[28] In practice, however, parametric modeling encompasses a much narrower range of factors than either the old programming matrices or a typical architect's intuitive decision making.[29] Parametrics can effectively model only *quantitative* characteristics. Parametric models leave aside the qualitative and unmeasurable things considered by architects during the design process that make for a complete work of architecture. Presumably these intransitive considerations will be dealt with outside the parametric modeling process.

This is why parametric models are not yet generally used to design buildings, but instead to design *parts of* buildings. For example, parametric modeling can be used to determine the configuration of roof trusses for an irregularly shaped roof. Nicholas Grimshaw and Partners' design of a roof structure at Waterloo International Rail Terminal (1994) is often cited as an early successful application of parametric processes. The design objectives for whole buildings are usually less well defined and less quantifiable. There are often contradictory design goals, with competing interests between the various users of a building, or even conflict between the building's owner and the rest of society. Design decisions aimed at maximizing the return on the client's investment may contradict other design decisions that would increase the building's benefits to the city around it. Such programmatic complexities defy the unambiguous (mathematical) definitions that parametric modeling requires.

Engineers Lead the Way

The parametric modeling process is borrowed from engineering disciplines such as aerospace engineering in which the design goals—minimizing weight for example—are tightly controlled and seldom controversial. Engineers often employ various parametric "form-finding strategies" in their design processes.[30] Once the range or field of forms is adequately narrowed, a process called "design optimization" can be used to refine the final form. Once again, the difficulty with transferring these strategies to the practice of architecture is that some design parameters are easier to incorporate into a model than others. Just as with BIM, shapes are much easier to represent mathematically than (for example) material properties, environmental characteristics, and aspects of a building's context. Many natural building materials have flaws, grain directions, inconsistent densities, and other characteristics that cannot be anticipated by modeling software. A building's social context may be even more challenging. How, for example, can a regional tradition of craft be accommodated in a process of which the ultimate end is the repositioning of all creative activity from the construction site to the architect's workstation?

In a typical engineering design process, "design parameters over which the designer has no control or that are too difficult to control" are excluded as "noise factors," since to address them would be to bog down the design process.[31] An architect's response to such noise factors, even if symbolic rather than performative, might actually contribute to a meaningful architectural project. A potential drawback to parametric modeling is that it may promote a kind of functionalist literalism in the design process. Before they emulate engineers too closely, architects need to consider that few engineers devote attention to what their projects signify. Parametric modeling remains best suited to organize technical knowledge related to a building's geometry or construction system. The ease (or difficulty) of transforming certain kinds of knowledge into "information" is one of the limiting factors Kolarevic's information master builders must face.

Advocates of parametric design point out that it allows designers to juggle more complex variables than the human mind can handle on its own. Anticipating this situation more than three decades ago, Nicholas Negroponte wrote,

> A machine, meanwhile, could procreate forms that respond to many heretofore unmanageable dynamics. Such a colleague would not be an omen to professional retirement but rather a tickler of the architect's imagination, presenting alternatives of form possibly not visualized or not visualizable by the human designer.[32]

Using computers to aid the designer's decision-making, rather than to simply represent designs worked out by other methods, is unquestionably a step forward for the profession.

Renewed architectural interest in engineering design processes is also promoting a closer collaborative relationship between the two disciplines. Yet this step does not come without its price. Engineers have been using methods similar to parametrics much longer than architects. Some engineers now claim that their profession's reliance on computers for design decision-making has cut them off from more immediate understanding of the consequences of their actions.[33]

Advantages and Limitations of Parametric Modeling

Much of the interest in parametric processes within engineering is fueled by the hope of increasing the speed of product design and development. Most architects do not share this wish to see the time available for design compressed even further. Architectural design is an attractive activity precisely because it is enjoyable (and, some might argue, necessary) to pursue over time. There is a limit to how far we can go toward making architectural design efficient and its outcomes certain without losing the reason most architects choose their profession in the first place. Furthermore, there is another path to alternatives of form "not visualizable by the human designer" and that is through the sorts of alterations to the basic design intention that are made by skilled craftspeople working in real time with real materials.

The inventiveness that architects associate with vernacular buildings comes from this kind of improvisational imaginative activity that cannot be foreseen. Concurrent with the revival of the architecture profession's interest in engineering has come a renewed interest in hands-on building processes. Auburn University's design-build Rural Studio sparked the imaginations of architecture students, who are now demanding the sorts of experiences that promote a direct, tactile understanding of building materials and processes. What is hopeful in this is that students do not view digital design techniques and hands-on construction as mutually exclusive. We believe there are as yet unrealized opportunities to combine these ways of working, as Foster and Partners has done with its Chesa Futura project (2004) in St. Moritz, Switzerland; the shape of this building was generated

Fig. 1 / Chesa Futura apartment building, Foster and Partners, St. Moritz, Switzerland, 2004

using parametric techniques, but it is clad in traditional hand-split cedar shingles.[34] [Fig. 1]

Another interesting nuance to the sorts of buildings or parts of buildings that have been designed using parametrics is that any technique that makes it easier and less expensive to construct complex irregular shapes will inevitably lead to a more widespread use of these kinds of shapes. This phenomenon is aptly described by Jim Rasenberger in *High Steel*:

> Why so much complexity? The short answer is economics and computers. Building owners wanted flexible, multiuse, tenant-pleasing spaces, and they wanted to build them as cheaply as possible. This is how they made their profits. Architects and engineers naturally wanted to satisfy their clients. Computers helped them do this by allowing them to measure loads and strains before any material was raised. They gave engineers the freedom to experiment and innovate

in ways that would have been inconceivable back in the 1920s. But if computers were facilitators to innovative engineers, they were also enablers to capricious and needy clients. The more complicated a building could be, the more complicated, inevitably, it *would* be.[35]

This suggests that our profession's newfound computer-aided ability to build geometrically complex buildings may become an addiction for some. Systematic design methods borrowed from engineering bring with them the engineering profession's focus on the wants of a relatively single-minded consumer. But should architects focus too heavily on satisfying capricious clients, particularly when architects have an ethical responsibility to advocate for those other than the client who will use, see, or indirectly support a project? While it is natural for any new building technology to have its experimental phase, this leads us to ask: how many buildings really need to be as geometrically complex as Frank Gehry's monumental projects? More important, what happens when clients or building producers start to question this complexity (or for that matter, to question whether engineers working with builders would even need architects on their design team)? What happens when developers decide that the cachet of a star architect like Gehry is unnecessary for their projects? Even though digital technology can be used to make our most important buildings less expensive, cannot similar technologies also be used to make "ordinary" buildings even cheaper and simpler? Kieran and Timberlake recognize this as a potential problem, when they write about "automating mediocrity," yet they do not convincingly explain how this situation is to be avoided.[36]

Helping and Hindering the Imagination

The great advantages of parametric modeling are its speed and unpredictability. It allows designers the opportunity to explore a far greater range of geometric options (some of which may be quite surprising, since a small quantitative change to a parameter may have a disproportionate effect on the shape of what is being modeled) than has previously been possible within a given time frame. Although one might argue that the imagination of an architect is capable of infinite options and variations, the speed with which parametric modeling processes work cannot really be matched without a computer.[37] Artists and designers have always been intrigued by variations on particular themes, and architectural educators have forever exhorted their students to explore multiple design solutions before selecting one. Parametrics allows designers to consider a myriad of detailed versions of a design, with any version poised to be fabricated using CNC technologies. Some designers call it "versioning." According to the talented New York firm Sharples Holden Pasquarelli (SHoP), "Versioning implies the shifting of design away from a system of horizontal integration (designers as simply the generators of representational form) towards a system of vertical integration (designers driving how space is conceived and constructed and what its cultural effects are)."[38]

While this statement may be an accurate description of what SHoP hopes to achieve through its parametric processes, it strikes us as something of an overstatement if applied to parametrics generally. The role of the designer who selects among the versions, who tweaks the design parameters, or introduces design considerations not strictly within the bounds of parametric modeling must not be overlooked. The architect's imagination remains the tool most useful to determine what a project's effects are culturally. Ironically, the impetus behind some of the exaggerated claims we find in the literature on this subject may be the unintentional result of the quality of the architects who are at the forefront of using these technologies. In the hands of top-notch designers like those at SHoP, Foster and Partners, KieranTimberlake, or Office dA, *any* design tool would produce positive results.

To the extent that parametric design methods lessen the architect's dependence on fixed formal strategies, parametrics will indeed expand the possibilities considered by architects in their design processes. By forcing the designers to describe unambiguous mathematical relationships, parametrics impose discipline on the architect's decision-making process. This "discipline" is a function of the distance parametrics inserts between the designer and the final form of any design. As the quote from SHoP implies, this distance may inspire designers to think beyond "representational form." Should this discipline also influence the architect to abandon "noisy" factors in favor of readily described geometric relationships, the long-term benefit of parametric design for architecture will be questionable. Furthermore, because the design issues that lend themselves to parametric processes are relatively narrow, they may merely lead to a formalism driven by the apparent search for performance replacing one propelled by the desire for "representational form." To an architect dedicated foremost to controlling form, parametric modeling could be manipulated to achieve the designer's intended idiosyncratic result under the guise of meeting the client's performance goals.[39]

Mass Customization

Joining the ability to generate multiple versions with the businessperson's wish for more nimble reactions to market forces leads us to the third innovation: mass customization. In his 1987 book, *Future Perfect*, Stanley M. Davis first used the term *mass customization*, supplying both a name and a conceptual framework for processes then taking hold in the clothing industry. Davis recognized that mass customizing simply extended the capabilities latent in all CAD/CAM processes. At about the same time Davis was writing, what would become the most often-referenced success story of mass customization was getting underway—Dell's use of mass customization in the sale and manufacture of personal computers.[40]

In 1993, B. Joseph Pine II expanded on Davis's ideas with *Mass Customization: The New Frontier in Business Competition*. Pine separated production into three categories: craft production, mass production, and mass customization, which combined elements of the first two.[41] Since Pine's initial writings on the subject, mass-customization techniques have matured so that most products produced this way (including Dell computers) combine some mass-produced components, often a "product platform," with others tailored to the customer's exact wishes.[42] Another key strategy for successful mass customization is modularization. "[P]roducts are 'decomposed' into modular components or subsystems that can be recombined to more nearly satisfy consumer needs."[43]

Myopic Customization, Without Social, Cultural, and Political Contexts

Like most authors (including architects) who have written on the subject, both Davis and Pine analyzed production solely in terms of its output. They did not study the social, cultural, and political effects of mass customization other than its advantages for business and direct benefits to consumers. To their credit, Kieran and Timberlake are willing to speculate on the future of, for example, labor unions in the brave new world of efficient building production. But their emphasis on "the improved working conditions" factory-built buildings may offer, and statements such as "union labor can be used just as readily when architecture is built inside the building as when it is built outside" strike us as naive.[44] Much of the political and economic power of skilled-tradesmen and women rests with the limited supply of their skills. Once these skills are made obsolete, the people who hold them are made interchangeable parts of the production process.

Kieran and Timberlake also miss the virtue of vernacular or craft production entirely. *Refabricating Architecture* looks at a quilting bee and concludes that the quilters are simply "assemblers."[45] In most that is written on this subject, the real fate of craftwork is ignored.[46] The demise of the skilled craftsperson is one instance in the ongoing transfer of economic and political power from those who work with their hands to the privileged class of "symbolic analysts" who manipulate information.[47] In a lecture to the architecture department at Pennsylvania State University, Stephen Kieran defended this process, saying that no plumber enjoys spending his days standing in sewage.[48] What this answer overlooks is that skilled workers have historically valued autonomy far more than physical comfort.[49]

This results-oriented instrumental mindset usually taints the "customization" part of mass customization too. Advocates of mass customization take "custom" to mean merely "one of a kind"—another example of removing something from its social context. A more common understanding of "custom" in our society is "rare, hard to obtain, and usually the work of craft-based production." Mass customization proposes to make custom goods available to everyone at nearly the same price as mass-produced goods—a noble goal perhaps, but one that would alter our society's understanding of what it means to have something "custom made." As currently practiced, mass customization allows the consumer to choose among a series of specific options, but these choices are far from infinite. Typically, this is because the consumer isn't really involved in the fundamental design decisions;

the consumer's preferences are not introduced until product fabrication. To create the final "custom" product one must work within a set of givens—think about how you build your new Dell computer online. There are always a finite number of custom computers that can be constructed.

While it is commonplace to hear that "mass customization" is an oxymoron, this observation misses the real contradiction of the concept in architectural practices. Most architecture, and nearly all designed by professional architects, is by its very nature "custom." The term *mass customization* brings to architecture only one idea not already inherent in its practices—"mass." Looked on in this light, it becomes questionable whether mass customization is all that different from previous attempts to industrialize building design and production. Architectural practices usually involve the consumer from the beginning of the process, so one of the main benefits of mass customization is already a part of the architect's traditional working methods. This process of working through a design project with an architect can be extremely time-consuming for the client. Ironically, the area of building production most likely to lend itself to mass customization, housing, is also the area where most consumers reject the limitless range of choices hiring an architect would afford them. In the design of their houses, it appears that most Americans prefer a limited range of options.[50] Designers too, have reasons to limit consumer choices. As one article on this subject states, "Imagine if someone chose a square headlight option on the vw bug, or asked for an iMac in matte black."[51]

Mass customization is founded on the belief that most customers want the ability to select the features of the products they purchase. In theory, if each customer can have exactly what he or she wants without paying a substantial premium for it, then each customer becomes a "market of one." As we have mentioned above, in practice mass customization generally falls short of the theoretical promise of true customization. Consumers are given a wide range of choices in *some* areas (say, the size, proportions, and color of a shirt), but lack the ability to redesign the product in most others (to create new fabric blends or entirely new shirt designs). So far, we have seen few examples in which mass customization provides a range of choices equal to that customers might have if they engaged the services of a skilled craftsperson.

From the organizational standpoint, since it is impossible to predict what each individual may want in a customized product, corporations practicing mass customization value flexibility. Mass customization marries the ability to create many versions of a product with an organizational structure that has "or can acquire the capabilities to give customers what they want."[52] The extent to which architectural firms have reacted to such market trends can today be seen primarily in the fluid alliances architectural firms make with other specialists in order to pursue particular projects. For one project a firm may partner with a star architect; for another it may align itself with a construction manager to pursue design-build opportunities.

Increased Choices for Architects, Designers, and Consumers

Where mass customization should benefit architects is by holding down the cost of one-of-a kind building components. Unlike some consumers, most designers *do* prefer to have a wide variety of choices. The ideal "consumer" of mass-customized building components may be the architect, not the building owner. This supposition is borne out by the fact that the most successful users of mass customization in the building industry are the producers of building components such as windows and curtain-wall systems. Andersen Corporation, makers of residential windows, has been using digital fabrication and mass customization since the early 1990s. Since updating its design and production methods this way, Andersen has seen exponential growth in the demand for custom "feature windows."[53] That said, the range of options an architect can expect from Andersen still falls short of what could be achieved, no doubt at greater expense, by working with a skilled carpenter or glazier.

Other promising applications for mass customization in buildings are those parts that are either repetitive or somewhat machine-like and therefore ripe for standardization, but that are still counted among the architectural features of the building. Restrooms, elevator cabs, kitchens, doors, railings, and stairways all satisfy one or both of these criteria. In one of the more convincing portions of *Refabricating Architecture,* Kieran and Timberlake describe their firm's designs for modular vanities, restrooms, and an addition to a collegiate residence hall.[54] We suspect that these readily modularized components and building types will indeed be the places where mass customization soon becomes an accepted part of architectural and construction practice.

Reducing Difficulty in the Making of Architecture

The promise of mass customization and architecture's adoption of computerized manufacturing techniques is a higher quality building at lower cost. According to *Refabricating Architecture*, architectural production will become a realm "where quality and scope can increase out of all proportion to cost and time, where art transcends resources."[55] The difficulty of producing architecture will be diminished by reordering practice around "information." *Refabricating Architecture* is unfailingly optimistic (as manifestos must be) about the possibilities of information technology and factory-based construction. Most of the literature on this subject agrees in principle with Kieran and Timberlake, predicting the architect's greater control over all aspects of a building project and heralding the return of "master builders."[56]

The implementation of technology, however, is never wholly positive, never without unintended and often negative consequences. Mies van der Rohe said that God is in the details, and architectural theorist Marco Frascari has written that details are the primary unit of architectural signification, the place where "construction and construing" are united.[57] If these statements are correct, what happens if we adopt methods of building fabrication dedicated to the elimination of costly details? A typical industrial method for reducing cost is to minimize the number of parts in a product. Add to this that CNC fabrication and rapid prototyping processes have an inherent bias toward monolithic materials. These fabrication techniques, the former subtractive and the latter additive, work best when the material being milled or deposited is of uniform density. What is often missed in discussions about the nearly unlimited ability of digital fabrication processes to create any shape is the corresponding reduction in the variety of fabrication methods and the range of materials utilized. There is no such thing as digitally fabricated wrought iron. Coupled with the economic advantages of building with fewer but larger modular "chunks," does this suggest that building technology, following the COMPUTABILITY = CONSTRUCTABILITY equation, is leading us to buildings with fewer details and less variety in the ways they are made?

Diminishing Details

At the end of *Refabricating Architecture*, Kieran and Timberlake describe a provocative experiment they pursued in their firm. They redesigned Mies's Farnsworth House (1951) using composite materials and modular construction. Rather than the 1,267 parts Kieran and Timberlake say needed to be individually assembled in the Farnsworth House, their value engineered version "reduced the overall number of parts assembled on site to somewhere between 22 and 48 components." They continue,

> GRP [glass reinforced plastic] was substituted for concrete and steel components wherever possible to lighten the overall weight of the structure, add durability, and increase [pre]assembly opportunities. By making substitutions for conventional materials with new, contemporary materials, the overall weight of the structure was reduced by 60 percent.[58]

An obvious question is why this new building—constructed of "new, contemporary materials"—would still look exactly like the Farnsworth House, for wouldn't adherence to the shape of the Farnsworth House put an arbitrary and unnecessary restriction on the performance of these new materials and construction procedures? On the other hand, can technology really help us diminish the difficulty of constructing a Farnsworth House without affecting its status as an architectural achievement?

One of the most notable details on the original Farnsworth House is the invisible connection between the steel columns and the horizontal steel channels that form the spandrel beams at the house's floor and deck levels. [Fig.2] The column supports the beam structurally, but there is no evidence that they are connected—no bolts, rivets, or visible welds. It is as if the two structural elements are joined only by magnetic force. Mies achieved this invisible connection by means of a

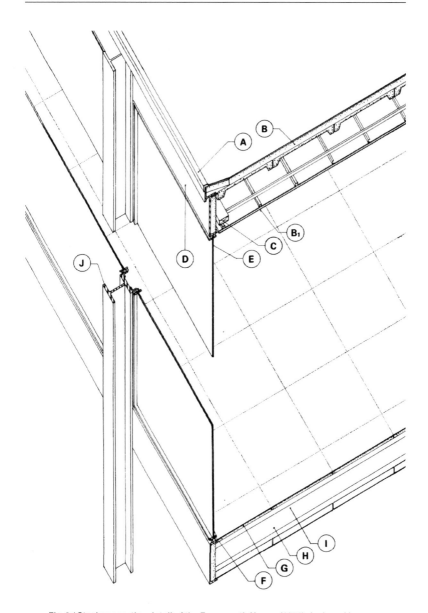

Fig. 2 / Steel connection detail of the Farnsworth House (1951) designed by
Mies van der Rohe, from Edward R. Ford, *The Details of Modern Architecture,
Volume 1*, 1996

plug weld. Each of the columns had a small slot cut in its flange where it met the spandrel. Welders filled in the slots with built-up weld material, which structurally joined the two pieces of steel. The plug welds were then ground smooth, flush with the flange of the columns, and painted. Mies and the welders covered their tracks, producing a detail that hides in plain sight.

Part of what makes this detail interesting, even for the casual observer who is not an architect or structural engineer, is that most people have a sense of the weight of steel. We also understand intuitively that steel connections are usually substantial and therefore visible. This was even more the case when the Farnsworth House was designed and built. At the typical highway-bridge or steel-building connection, one was likely to see a jumble of rivets or bolts. To take away the steel and its weight is to render this particular detail meaningless. In this instance, the architecture loses weight in both the physical and metaphorical senses.

Difficulty as Source of Architectural Value

Much written about the impact of these digital techniques on the profession claims that they are making it less difficult to create architecture. Yet there are those of us who believe that difficulty has *in itself* essential cultural value for architecture. Without some form of resistance—material, climatic, economic, social—there is no way to measure architectural achievement. The philosopher Gaston Bachelard once proposed that all human accomplishment could be assessed against an ambiguous scale he called the "Coefficient of Adversity."[59] While the Coefficient cannot be applied transitively—it is not a quantifiable variable—it suggests that what we tend to value most are those things that are difficult to achieve.

In architecture there is an age-old connection between complexity and difficulty. Buildings that have been very complex to construct, often because of their size and shape, have usually been the most important buildings in any culture. (Mies's "less is more" approach only appeared to contradict this relationship. His buildings seemed simple until one began to appreciate how they had been constructed.) Part of what has historically conditioned the public to *receive* a new work of architecture is the familiarity they have had with it during its erection. It is much harder to dislike a building if two generations of your ancestors helped create it. While this form of socialization has been slowly disappearing since the nineteenth century, architectural production has resisted industrialization far longer than most other manufacturing.

Digital fabrication techniques promise to drastically alter the long-standing difficulty/complexity relationship, while further reducing the time available to socialize the public to a new building. Rapid-prototyping machines can make models of any object, almost without regard for its geometric complexity, and full-scale digital fabrication is only a few steps behind. The more industrialized architectural production becomes, the more architecture, like all other consumer goods, must rely on marketing techniques to prepare it for public acceptance.

There are real differences between the goals of architects and engineers, differences that much of the current discourse ignores. As technologists, engineers are trained to confront difficulty head on. Also, engineers have a less contentious relationship with economics than architects. Since contemporary economics conceptualizes the global economy as a machine, the goals of engineers and economists have to some degree merged. The word *economy* has been instrumentalized, so that at the process level, *economy* and *efficiency* are practically interchangeable. Engineers seldom question the goal of increased efficiency, since to do so is to no longer remain a technologist. To the architect, efficiency/economy is a double-edged sword. An architect who ignores efficiency designs wasteful buildings. An architect who slavishly serves efficiency produces affordable but uninspiring buildings. Rather than eradicating difficulty in the service of economy, good architects try to engage difficulty in meaningful ways. Mies wasn't trying to design the most efficient joint between a column and beam at the Farnsworth House. He was trying to create a detail that "told tales." A building without details, with too few parts, would be *inarticulate*. Articulation, after all, demands the presence of joints.

For years, practicing architects have been criticizing architecture schools for inadequate business education in their curricula. Now we see ideas that originated in business, such as mass customization, being imported directly and uncritically into architectural schools and practices. This is also true of engineering-based techniques like parametric modeling. We believe that BIM, parametric modeling, and mass customization each has potential to impact architecture and its practice in positive ways, but they should not be adapted uncritically. Manifestos and marketing slogans are hollow. Advances in digital design and fabrication must now be placed in the broader context of architectural theory and criticism.

Digital Master Builders

Since the Renaissance, European and American architects have steadily influenced less of the design and construction process. This diminution has accelerated in our own time with the increasing complexity of buildings and the fragmentation of building design into the work of more and more disciplines. The idea that architects can reclaim control over building projects is therefore attractive to most of us, appealing not only to our egos but also to our instinct for self-preservation. Although architects have continually given up (or lost) control of elements of building design and construction, we have fought to hold onto form as our last stronghold. Architecture students, magazines, and probably most practicing architects believe that the architect's primary job is to create form. Parametric modeling software "automatically" generates forms based on data input by the operator of the computer.[60] Such a process requires that the architect give up control of form to a computer-generated algorithm to regain control in areas where it has been lost to other professions. We would argue that, in order for the process to be successful, the architect's active participation is necessary; there is nothing "automatic" about it.

The idea that architects should take more control of the construction process misses another important aspect of the creation of architecture. Architecture is, now as much as ever, a collaborative endeavor. There is an irreducible aspect of ceremony to all construction projects. Just as more is happening at a quilting bee than the stitching of fabric, more takes place on a construction site than assembling the building parts specified by an architect. During construction, contractors and tradespeople use their experience to orchestrate the work, resolve joints between materials, and accommodate conditions that resist the architect's documentation. Increasing the architect's control over construction and reducing the input by skilled builders is no guarantee that the results will be more successful (although they may be more *certain*). Material resistance can best be overcome by those who are accustomed to working with specific materials. Whether the architect is sharing control with a contractor or acquiring craft skills himself, the improvisational give-and-take between a design intention and its realization is likely to lead to better architecture than a "perfect" execution of a designer's intentions. Digital design tools can be used to enhance collaboration as easily as they enhance control. The relationship Frank Gehry's office has developed with steel fabricators is a case in point.

The Promise of Economical Complexity

Techniques that make something easier to obtain or achieve inevitably reduce the cultural importance of that thing. Luckily, this does not mean that the best buildings are only those that are prohibitively expensive and difficult to construct. The Coefficient of Adversity is not something that can be quantified in this manner. The best architecture always embraces difficulty on some level, and the need to economize is one of architecture's most commonly encountered difficulties. Yet architecture cannot simply accept the transitive measure of the accountant's bottom line. Architecture finds its economy not by relentlessly cutting back or through value engineering, but by cleverly using materials in unexpected ways, by reconceptualizing the client's program so that one space serves multiple purposes to the benefit of them all, and by engaging the imaginations of those who occupy it so that there is more to architecture than what is physically present in a building. Most of what has been written about the latest digital techniques for designing and fabricating architecture ignores these admittedly slippery distinctions and instead adopts without question the language and concepts of engineering or business. In this, we should heed the words of architectural theorist Dalibor Vesely: "Because architects are not usually much concerned with the sources and the nature of knowledge received from other fields, tending to view it either uncritically or as a pragmatic tool, they are very often the victims of deep confusion."[61]

There may also be instances—disaster relief housing for example—when architecture with a capital A is less vital than safe,

affordable shelter. It is in these areas that more-efficient building production technologies can potentially have the greatest impact. We
would argue, however, that the work of architects such as Shigeru Ban
and the Rural Studio demonstrate that the ambition to create architecture is compatible even with the need for basic shelter. The architectural profession must now begin coming to terms with the shifting
relationship between complexity and customization in the context of
diminished architectural difficulty. We see signs that some firms are
making these sorts of adjustments to their digital practices. SHoP,
for example—in projects such as the P.S.1 Dunescape (2000), the
Virgin Atlantic Clubhouse (2004) at JFK International Airport, and the
Mitchell Park buildings (2001) on the waterfront in Greenport, New
York—seems to be searching for (and finding) an appropriate yet economical complexity, one tailored to particular materials and building
techniques. The Dunescape was made up of thousands of cedar two-
by-twos. This resulted in a permeable surface that would allow in light
and air. As in the traditional masonry building, the Dunescape's joints
were all visible, allowing viewers to appreciate the resonance between
its shape and its medium of construction. [Fig.3] In addition, architectural theorists such as Patrick Harrop have begun to investigate ways
to "embed" resistance into digital architectural production.[62]

These are encouraging signs, and there are others. In 2004
Stephen Kieran lectured at Pennsylvania State to a large audience of
architecture students, uncharacteristically joined by many engineering faculty and students. Few left the room during either the long lecture or the forty-five minutes of questions after it. Like *Refabricating
Architecture*, Kieran's lecture was unfailingly positive, and the students seemed inspired. At a discussion during the University of
Pennsylvania conference on which Kolarevic's book was based, architect Sulan Kolatan stated, "The last time there was this much joy and
optimism in architecture was probably in the 1960s." She is right. And
in spite of its tendency to oversimplify, *Refabricating Architecture* is
a book every architect should read. Kieran and Timberlake have aided
the profession by challenging its attachment to practices rooted in
obsolete technologies. Yet the rest of Kolatan's statement should not
be swept away by this tsunami of optimism: "It seems to me that we
are in danger of falling into some of the same holes that the 1960s

Fig. 3 / P.S.1 Dunescape, SHoP Architects, Long Island City, Queens,
New York, 2000

generation fell into. One of them is perhaps an extreme reliance on
technology. We ought to be careful about trusting a new technology to
create perfect solutions on its own."[63] This article has been our attempt
to begin implementing Kolatan's advice.

Postscript

Obviously, by writing about an area as fast-moving as digital technology, we knew that our original assessment of the "state of the art" in
2005 would be short-lived. The three main techniques we described—
BIM, parametric modeling, and mass customization—have all developed since. BIM, in particular, is now seemingly ubiquitous and is used
to some degree in nearly all architecture firms today, although mainly
in ways that fall far short of its potential. Nevertheless, we believe that
many of our comments, both positive toward and critical of these techniques continue to apply.

"Diminishing difficulty" still seems to be the primary motivation for most of the developers and end-users of these techniques. If anything, our critique of the limitations of this positivistic mind-set would be even stronger today. We could have said more about the misfit between the actual construction practices and the inherent tendencies of software and other digital tools. (Exploration of these tendencies and limitations of software could be the subject of another, equally long article.)

We are now perhaps better positioned to comment on the lack of details and detailing (in the sense Marco Frascari uses the term) in many current projects. If one adopts Frascari's stance that architectural details are the architects' primary means of signification on any project, then the economically driven, positivistic pursuit to eliminate component parts and reduce the number of joints in a typical building is called into question. Here we have an instance of architects willingly eliminating the expressive opportunities from their own work.

There is a "literalness" about the ways architects are using digital representation and simulation techniques that ignores a whole class of nonliteral, nonprojective means of representation. Dalibor Vesely calls these "symbolic representations," and Frascari refers to them as "demonstrations." Like drama and fiction, demonstrative drawings may reveal something true through absence or exaggeration. These sorts of drawings have always been an essential part of the architect's tool kit, but they are becoming forgotten as the power of digital techniques to accurately model the geometry of complex shapes continues to improve. We would argue that the digital tools now at the architect's disposal have great, but as yet untapped, potential in this realm.

By adopting not only the tools, but the language from business, engineering, and information technology, architects may be forgetting what is unique and most creative about traditional manners of working.

Ivan Illich referred to this phenomenon broadly as the "industrial corruption of language" and wrote about the limitations imposed when expression is restricted. Vesely warns us of the danger in "subordinating all knowledge and different ways of making to instrumental rationality and technology." Within and around architectural discourse, today's favorite buzzword may be "smart." We have smart materials, smart structures, smart drawings, smart spaces. We are suspicious that "smartness" may not encompass the complete range of humanistic goals native to architecture.

Given the penchant for architects, and our society, to uncritically adopt new techniques and the latest gadget that promises to diminish difficulty, we believe that our conclusion to the original essay is something that bears repeating. If these techniques of architectural production are not critically examined, we run the risk of losing our way as architects. Instead, we ought to be looking for ways to imaginatively incorporate such techniques into our design processes. New technologies can't guarantee better architecture, however, talented architects thoughtfully and critically employing these technologies could surprise all of us.

Dan Willis is an architect, professor, and head of the Department of Architecture at Pennsylvania State University. He is the author of numerous articles and books including *The Emerald City and Other Essays on the Architectural Imagination* (Princeton Architectural Press, 1999).

Todd Woodward is a principal of SMP Architects in Philadelphia and adjunct assistant professor in the architecture department of the Tyler School of Art at Temple University.

Notes

1 Stephen Kieran and James Timberlake, *Refabricating Architecture* (New York: McGraw Hill, 2004), xiii.

2 "Choice Cut: SHoP Serves up Digital Fabrication in New York's Meatpacking District," *Architecture*, June 2004, 74–81.

3 Bruce Lindsey, *Digital Gehry* (Basel: Birkhäuser, 2001), 84.

4 Greg Lynn, *Animate Form* (New York: Princeton Architectural Press, 1999).

5 IT Revolution was the title of a popular series of books edited by Antonio Saggio and published by Birkhäuser in 2000 and 2001.

6 For readers too young to recall this period, systems drafting techniques attempted to minimize wasted manual drawing time by using multiple layers of drafting film—one layer for the structural grid, one for the walls, one for the electrical layout, etc.—and then sandwiching these together on a flat bed printer to form composite drawings. For buildings with multiple repetitive floors, this could, for instance, save the time that was previously spent redrawing the structural grid for each floor. The drawings were kept in perfect alignment through punched holes in the drafting film through which a pin bar was inserted. This is exactly the same layering process most CAD programs use, but the drawings were still drafted by hand.

7 *Building information modeling* is a generic term, similar to a number of terms trademarked by competing software manufacturers. The Autodesk products Architectural Desktop and Revit, Bentley's MicroStation TriForma, and ArchiCAD by Graphisoft all promise these advances to varying degrees.

8 Branko Kolarevic, "Digital to Material," lecture at Pennsylvania State University, February 17, 2005.

9 C. C. Sullivan, "Brace for BIM," *Architecture*, April 2005, 77–80.

10 The AIA Technology in Architectural Practice Advisory Group.

11 Branko Kolarevic, ed., *Architecture in the Digital Age: Design and Manufacturing* (New York: Spon Press, 2003), v.

12 Robin Evans, "Translation from Drawing to Building," AA Files 12 (1986): 3–18.

13 Kolarevic, *Architecture in the Digital Age*, 31.

14 At the 2005 AIA Convention, a technology interest group of the AIA presented the inaugural "Building Information Model" awards.

15 Kieran and Timberlake, *Refabricating Architecture*, 61.

16 Charles Eastman, "New Methods of Architecture and Building," in *Fabrication: Examining the Digital Practice of Architecture*, ed. Philip Beesley, Nancy Yen-Wen Cheng, and R. Shane Williamson (Proceedings of the 2004 AIA/ACADIA Fabrication Conference, 2004), 21.

17 Since architects are seldom experts in construction sequencing, architects and contractors will be forced to collaborate to a greater extent than has been the case under the still popular "design-bid-build" system of project delivery. (We tend to agree with Kieran and Timberlake, Eastman, and Kolarevic that the dominance of design-bid-build will soon end.) BIMs may make errors in the design less likely, but they will not address the sequence of building operations unless a knowledgeable builder is involved, and the BIM becomes a "4-D model," incorporating the time of construction.

18 Bernard Cache, "Towards a Fully Associative Architecture" in *Architecture in the Digital Age*, 144.

19 See "The Contradictions Underlying the Practice of Architecture" in Dan Willis, *The Emerald City and Other Essays on the Architectural Imagination* (New York: Princeton Architectural Press, 1999).

20 Kolarevic, *Architecture in the Digital Age*, 11–27.

21 At the 2002 University of Pennsylvania conference on which Kolarevic's book is based, architect Sulan Kolatan answered the question, "Why aren't the differences more dramatic between the projects?" with "There is a kind of homogeneity that is the default condition of the software we use." Kolarevic, *Architecture in the Digital Age*, 295.

22 We should add that Kolarevic also mentions that curved forms are characteristic of broader product and industrial design culture, not only a phenomenon related to building design. Another consideration, however, is that a building, unlike all of these other designed objects, has a site to which it must respond. We wonder if, due to the difficultly of modeling topography, plantings, utilities, and other site characteristics, these limitations in our ability to model might lead to buildings designed with less regard for the uniqueness of their sites.

23 [Editor's note: The source of this statement is Farmingdale State College Professor of Mechanical and Manufacturing Engineering Ahmed Ibrahim. The website from which the authors cited this statement is no longer active.] http://info.lu.farmingdale.edu/profiles/ibrahiaz/211.htm.

24 Kolarevic, *Architecture in the Digital Age*, 17.

25 Alex Kilian, "Linking Digital Hanging Chain Models to Fabrication," *Fabrication: Examining the Digital Practice of Architecture*, 123.

26 Kolarevic, *Architecture in the Digital Age*, 18.

27 See, for example, Paul Laseau, *Graphic Problem Solving for Architects and Builders* (Boston: Cahners Publishing, 1975).

28 Timothy W. Simpson, Uwe Lautenschlager, and Farrokh Mistree, "Mass Customization in the Age of Information: The Case for Open Engineering Systems," *The Information Revolution: Current and Future Consequences* (Greenwich, CT: Ablex Publishing, 2000), 61.

29 See Anna Dyson, "Recombinant Assemblies," *Architectural Design* 72, no. 5 (2002): 63.

30 See J. J. Shah, and M. Mantyla, *Parametric and Feature-Based CAD/CAM* (New York: John Wiley & Sons, 1995).

31 Timothy W. Simpson, Jonathan R. Maier, and Farrokh Mistree, "Product Platform Design," *Research Engineering Design* 13, no. 1 (August 2001): 5; and G. Taguchi, E. A. Elsayad, and T. Hsiang, *Quality Engineering in Production Systems* (New York: McGraw-Hill, 1989).

32 Nicholas Negroponte, *The Architecture Machine* (Cambridge, MA: MIT Press, 1970), cited by Kolarevic, *Architecture in the Digital Age*, 21.

33 Eugene S. Fergusen, "How Engineers Lose Touch," *Invention and Technology*, Winter 1993, 16–24.

34 Hugh Whitehead, "Laws of Form," in Kolarevic, *Architecture in the Digital Age*, 98–100.

35 Jim Rasenberger, *High Steel: The Daring Men Who Built the World's Greatest Skyline* (New York: Harper Collins, 2004), 79.

36 Kieran and Timberlake, *Refabricating Architecture*, 112.

37 Parametric modeling treats the process of form generation as simple problem solving. What computers do poorly is to consider unprecedented ways of solving (or redefining) the problem. The computer doesn't think "outside the box." A talented designer is necessary for that.

38 Sharples Holden Pasquarelli, introduction to "Versioning: Evolutionary Techniques in Architecture," *Architectural Design* 72, no. 5 (2002): 8.

39 Kolarevic notes, "The challenge…is how to avoid a literal transcription of the diagrams…into an architectural form, as the superposition of datascapes, static or dynamic, often generates spatial and temporal constructs with apparent architectonic qualities." Kolarevic, *Architecture in the Digital Age*, 22.

40 E. Schonfeld, "The Customized, Digitized, Have-It-Your Way Economy," *Fortune*, September 1998, 115–24.

41 B. Joseph Pine II, *Mass Customization: The New Frontier in Business Competition* (Boston: Harvard Business School Press, 1993), 50–52.

42 Simpson et. al, "Product Platform Design."

43 Tim Crayton, "The Design Implications of Mass Customization," Design Intelligence, May 2001, http://www.di.net/articles/archive/2054.

44 Kieran and Timberlake, *Refabricating Architecture*, 123–25.

45 Ibid., 56.

46 For instance, Manuel DeLanda, in *A Thousand Years of NonLinear History* (New York: Zone Books, Swerve editions, 2000), 300, writes: "A full cost-benefit accounting of routinized, disciplinary operations needs to be performed not only in terms of economic utility but also in terms of political obedience."

47 The symbolic analyst label has been popularized by former Secretary of Labor Robert Reich.

48 Stephen Kieran, lecture to the Penn State University Department of Architecture, March 2004.

49 Joanne B. Ciulla, *The Working Life* (New York: Crown Business, 2000), 54–70; especially 69.

50 The consumer preference for a reassuringly limited range of choices goes beyond just the American homebuyers' preference for suburban McMansions. See: Barry Schwartz, *The Paradox of Choice: Why More is Less* (New York: Harper Collins, 2004).

51 Michael Chaoover, "Mass Customizi-Who—What Dell, Nike, & Others Have in Store for You," Core 77, http://www.core77.com/reactor/mass_customization.html.

52 B. Joseph Pine, Bart Victor, and Andrew C. Boynton, "Making Mass Customization Work," *Markets of One* (Boston: Harvard Business School Press, 2000), 166.

53 Tim Stevens, "More Panes, More Gains," *Industry Week*, December 18, 1995, 60.

54 Kieran and Timberlake, *Refabricating Architecture*, 136–53.

55 Ibid., 11.

56 The area of disagreement might be in the time frame within which this change will take place. Kieran and Timberlake apparently believe that it is imminent, whereas Kolarevic believes that it may take many years to overcome cultural and legal barriers to this reorganization of architectural practice.

57 Marco Frascari, *Monsters of Architecture* (Savage, MD: Rowman & Littlefield, 1991), 12.

58 Kieran and Timberlake, *Refabricating Architecture*, 171.

59 Gaston Bachelard, *Water and Dreams*, trans. Edith Farrell (Dallas, TX: The Dallas Institute, 1993), 159–61.

60 In "Digital Morphogenesis," Kolarevic writes, "Instead of modeling an external form, designers articulate an internal generative logic, which then produces, in automatic fashion, a range of possibilities from which the designer could choose an appropriate formal proposition for further development."

61 Dalibor Vesely, *Architecture in the Age of Divided Representation* (Cambridge, MA: MIT Press, 2004), 23.

62 Patrick Harrop, "Agents of Risk: Embedding Resistance in Architectural Production," *Fabrication*, 66–75.

63 Sulan Kolatan, quoted in *Architecture in the Digital Age*, 291.

Illustration Credits

Instrumental Geometry
Figs. 1–3: Courtesy Foster + Partners
Figs. 4–6: Courtesy KPF London

Using Building Information Modeling for Performance-based Design
Figs. 1–4: © Eddy Krygiel, courtesy Sybex

Innovate or Perish: New Technologies and Architecture's Future
Fig. 1: Courtesy Dr. Behrokh Khoshnevis, director, Center for Rapid Automated Fabrication Technologies (CRAFT), University of Southern California
Fig. 3: Courtesy of William Massie
Fig. 4: Courtesy of Christopher Deam
Fig. 5: Courtesy of Jones, Partners: Architecture
Fig. 6: Courtesy of Sulan Kolatan and William MacDonald, KOLMAC LLC

Complexity and Customization: The Porter House Condominium— SHoP Architects
Figs. 1–4: Courtesy of SHoP Architects

Remaking in a Postprocessed Culture
Figs. 1–4: Courtesy of William Massie

Engineering of Freeform Architecture
Fig. 1: Courtesy Bernhard Franken, ABB Architekten
Fig. 2: Courtesy Bollinger + Grohmann
Fig. 3: Courtesy Bollinger + Grohmann, Harry Schiffer
Fig. 4–5: Courtesy Harald Kloft, o-s-d
Fig. 6: Courtesy Bollinger + Grohmann
Fig. 7: Courtesy Harald Kloft, o-s-d
Fig. 8: Courtesy Harald Kloft, o-s-d, and Kuhn + Steinbächer Architekten

Self-organization and Material Constructions
Fig. 1: Shutterstock Images
Figs. 2–4: Courtesy of Arup+PTW+CCDI

Automation Takes Command: The Nonstandard, Unautomatic History of Standardization and Automation in Architecture
Fig. 1: Figures 141–43 and 147 from Charles Singer, E. J. Holmyard, and A. R. Hall, eds., *A History of Technology, Volume 1: From Early Times to Fall of Empires* (New York: Oxford University Press, 1954), 222–24, 226.
Fig. 2: Drawing by Kiel Moe based on an image from the Collections of the Division of Armed Forces History, National Museum of American History, Smithsonian Institution Neg. No. 62468
Fig. 3: Drawing by Kiel Moe based on figure 2.1 from J. Francis Reintjes, *Numerical Control: Making a New Technology* (New York, Oxford University Press, 1991), 30.
Fig. 4: Drawing by Kiel Moe based on figure 4.8 from J. Francis Reintjes, *Numerical Control: Making a New Technology* (New York, Oxford University Press, 1991), 88.

Diminishing Difficulty: Mass Customization and the Digital Production of Architecture
Fig. 1: Courtesy Nigel Young / Foster + Partners
Fig. 2: Ford, Edward R., *The Details of Modern Architecture, Volume 1*, figure 9.10 © Massachusetts Institute of Technology, by permission of The MIT Press.
Fig. 3: Courtesy of SHoP Architects

Achim Menges, "Instrumental Geometry," *Architectural Design* 76, no. 2 (2006): 42–53. Reproduced with permission of John Wiley & Sons, Ltd.

Portions of Eddy Krygiel, "Using Building Information Modeling for Performance-based Design" appeared in Eddy Krygiel and Brad Nies, *Green BIM: Successful Sustainable Design with Building Information Modeling* (Indianapolis: Sybex, 2008). Reproduced with permission.

David Celento, "Innovate or Perish: New Technologies and Architecture's Future," *Harvard Design Magazine* 26 (2007): 70–82. Reproduced with permission of the Harvard University Graduate School of Design.

André Chaszar and James Glymph, "CAD/CAM in the Business of Architecture, Engineering, and Construction," *Architectural Design* 73, no. 6 (2003): 117–23. Reproduced with permission of John Wiley & Sons, Ltd.

Amanda Reeser Lawrence, "Complexity and Customization: The Porter House Condominium—SHoP Architects," *PRAXIS*, no. 6 (2004): 46–53. Reproduced with permission.

William Massie, "Remaking in a Post-Processed Culture," *Architectural Design* 72, no. 5 (2002): 54–59. Reproduced with permission of John Wiley & Sons, Ltd.

Harald Kloft, "Engineering of Freeform Architecture," in *New Technologies in Architecture II & III: Digital Design and Manufacturing Techniques*, ed. Martin Bechthold, Kimo Griggs, Daniel L. Schodek, and Marco Steinberg (Cambridge, MA: Harvard University Graduate School of Design, 2003). Reproduced with permission of the Harvard University Graduate School of Design.

James Woudhuysen with Stephen Kieran and James Timberlake, "Mass Customisation and the Manufacture Module," *Architectural Design* 76, no. 1 (2006): 49–51. Reproduced with permission of John Wiley & Sons, Ltd.

Michael Weinstock, "Self-Organisation and Material Constructions," *Architectural Design* 76, no. 2 (2006): 34–41. Reproduced with permission of John Wiley & Sons, Ltd.

Martin Bechthold, "On Shells and Blobs: Structural Surfaces in the Digital Age," *Harvard Design Magazine* 19 (2003): 67–72. Reproduced with permission of the Harvard University Graduate School of Design.

Daniel Willis and Todd Woodward, "Diminishing Difficulty: Mass Customization and the Digital Production of Architecture," *Harvard Design Magazine* 23 (2005): 70–83. Reproduced with permission of the Harvard University Graduate School of Design.

Published by
Princeton Architectural Press
37 East 7th Street
New York, NY 10003

For a free catalog of books, call 1-800-722-6657
Visit our website at www.papress.com

© 2010 Princeton Architectural Press
All rights reserved
Printed and bound in Canada
13 12 11 10 4 3 2 1 First edition

No part of this book may be used or reproduced in any manner without written permission from the publisher, except in the context of reviews.

Every reasonable attempt has been made to identify owners of copyright. Errors or omissions will be corrected in subsequent editions.

Editor: Wendy Fuller
Designer: Paul Wagner

Special thanks to:
Nettie Aljian, Bree Anne Apperley, Sara Bader, Nicola Bednarek, Janet Behning, Becca Casbon, Carina Cha, Tom Cho, Penny (Yuen Pik) Chu, Carolyn Deuschle, Russell Fernandez, Pete Fitzpatrick, Wendy Fuller, Jan Haux, Nancy Eklund Later, Linda Lee, Laurie Manfra, John Myers, Katharine Myers, Steve Royal, Dan Simon, Andrew Stepanian, Jennifer Thompson, Joseph Weston, and Deb Wood of Princeton Architectural Press
—Kevin C. Lippert, publisher

Library of Congress Cataloging-in-Publication Data
Fabricating architecture : selected readings in digital design and manufacturing / Robert Corser, editor. — 1st ed.
    p.   cm.
Includes index.
ISBN 978-1-56898-889-4 (alk. paper)
1. Architecture and technology. 2. Architecture—Data processing. 3. Architecture—Technological innovations. 4. Architectural design. 5. Architectural practice. I. Corser, Robert. II. Title: Selected readings in digital design and manufacturing.
NA2543.T43F33 2010
720.285—dc22
                          2009035355

eISBN: 978-1-61689-000-1